PONDMASTER

An essential guide to choosing your

KOI
COLOUR VARIETIES

NICK FLETCHER

INTERPET PUBLISHING

Author

Nick Fletcher, former editor of the UK aquatic monthly Practical Fishkeeping, still regularly contributes articles to this and other fish-related publications. His interest in tropical and coldwater fishes stems from his lifelong hobby of angling, but nowadays he prefers keeping fish to catching them. Koi have been a principal interest since the mid-1970s; Nick is actively involved in his local koi club, and instead of a lawn he has a koi pond.

© 2002 Interpet Publishing,
Vincent Lane, Dorking, Surrey, RH4 3YX, England.
All rights reserved.
ISBN: 1-84286-064-X

Credits

Created and designed: Ideas into Print,
New Ash Green, Kent DA3 8JD, England.
Production management: Consortium, Poslingford,
Suffolk CO10 8RA, England.
Print production: Sino Publishing House Ltd., Hong Kong.
Printed and bound in China.

Below: Beautiful, challenging and infinitely rewarding, koi inspire a lifelong delight in all who keep them. A fish like this Gin-Rin Sanke is just one among hundreds of varieties available in all size and price brackets.

Contents

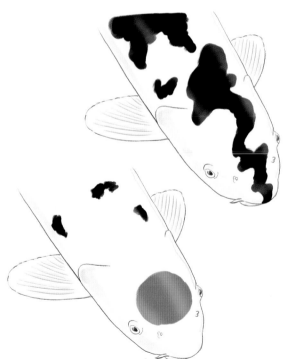

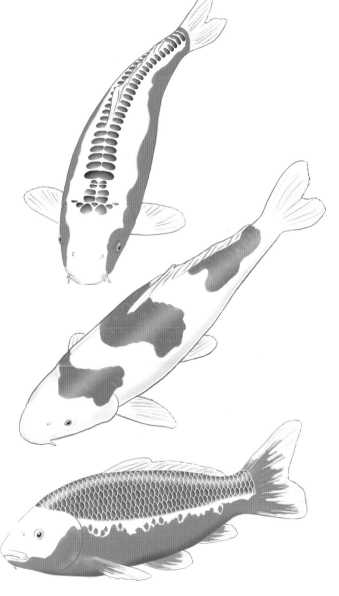

The obsession starts here

There are koi, and there are other pondfish. What makes koi so special? It is an affair of the heart, an inevitable passion that begins with your first sight of these 'living jewels' swimming in crystal-clear water. You cannot help but be captivated by their sparkling vitality, or marvel at their vivid colours as they rise to be hand-fed. Young koi have an energy all their own, and as they grow they develop a stately presence that goldfish can never aspire to.

Some people keep koi purely as pets, not too bothered where their fish come from or what they look like. Others start with this attitude, only to realise that the hobby is open-ended. Ponds are then speedily enlarged and upgraded to house quality Japanese fish, and books, magazines and websites are quickly devoured in a steep learning curve to absorb all the latest techniques and information.

At this stage, the best thing a koi-keeper can do is to join a club, where he or she will benefit from pooled experience. It's a social network, too, as clubs arrange talks, outings and shows, where members' fish are judged against one another. The next stage is the open show circuit, where koi can compete against the best in the land.

Koi-keeping has made huge advances in the past 20 years. In response to rising demand, a worldwide support industry of dealers, distributors and manufacturers has grown up to offer quality fish at reasonable prices. The enduring appeal of koi is that no two are alike. There are gaudy fish and subtle fish, koi with a full complement of scales and others that are almost scaleless. They may be metallic or matt or sparkling, of one colour or several. The impact of these colours, on an individual fish or in the company of others, determines the mood of the collection.

However you build your collection, healthy well-kept koi are a visual feast and a calming influence in today's fast-paced world. As a beginner, you may find learning to recognise the many varieties of koi and their Japanese names a challenge. This book will provide a valuable first step along the road to familiarisation, along with a brief history of koi and the basic know-how that you will need before you embark on this most fulfilling of hobbies.

All modern koi are descendants of carp (*Cyprinus carpio*), which are indigenous to the Black, Aral, Caspian and Azov Seas of Eastern Asia. The species is highly adaptable and a valuable human food source so, not surprisingly, it spread everywhere that armies marched – across mainland Europe with the Romans and into Britain with the Crusaders around 1550 AD.

The Chinese kept carp five centuries before the birth of Christ, accrediting the fish with near-mystical powers of tenacity. But the story of koi (which simply means 'carp' in Japanese) really began when Chinese forces invaded their island neighbours. Fish were released into the lakes and rivers of Japan, where they thrived – albeit at the expense of some native species, which they out-competed for food.

In the seventeenth century, the peasant rice farmers of Niigata in northern Japan began to culture the introduced Magoi (black carp), which they would dry and salt to sustain their families through the short, but severe, Japanese winters, when small mountain communities were invariably snowed in. The fish were raised in terraced irrigation reservoirs overlooking the paddy fields and harvested in October, before the snows arrived. Larger, parent carp were retained in ponds, some within the farmers' own houses.

The start of koi-keeping

In this sheltered environment, fish with colour abnormalities began to appear. Carp whose black pigment cells (melanophores) were deficient would show a few red or white scales. Instead of these conspicuous fish being picked off by predators, as would happen in the wild, the farmers crossed them with other mutants to fix these characteristics, purely for curiosity's sake. By the mid-nineteenth century these oddities had achieved pet status. As aquaculture methods improved, and merchants came to Niigata to buy the surplus food fish, the mysterious 'coloured carp' became an open secret among Japan's moneyed classes, who became the first true koi-keepers.

Left: These portly Magoi, or black carp, started it all. Scale mutations arising from inbreeding among fish for the table have resulted in the many colourful, impressive koi varieties we know today.

Right: Koi-keeping is also about creating an Oriental ambience. This Japanese garden blends lanterns, pagodas and stylised planting with the all-important rock pond. Scaled-down versions can be seen worldwide.

The wider commercial possibilities of koi in their new ornamental role were realised at the 1914 Taisho Exhibition in Tokyo, when 27 coloured carp were publicly displayed. Afterwards, some were gifted to the Emperor for his palace moat, while others were bought by enterprising individuals who guessed there was more money to be made from live fish than dead ones.

It is not certain when koi first arrived in the USA, but the 1941 World Fair in San Francisco featured a large pond of these fish in a Japanese pavilion. Hawaii received its first shipment in 1947. Not until the mid-1960s did koi become available in the UK,

largely through the efforts of a fishkeeping businessman who dug holding lakes and teamed up with the owner of a Birmingham-based aquatics outlet to import the fish from the Japanese farmer, Kamihata. With improved air transport and the invention of the plastic bag, which has played a vital role in the successful transportation of koi, this trickle of fish into the UK quickly became a flood.

The modern hobby

In half a century, the quality of Japanese koi has improved immeasurably, with new varieties being developed and existing ones refined. There are metallic koi, plain or multicoloured; partially-scaled Doitsu fish (resulting from crosses with German mirror carp originally bred for the table); Gin-Rin koi with sparkling scales and, most importantly for the true koi devotee, superb modern examples of the 'Big Three' varieties – Kohaku, Sanke and Showa, collectively known as Go Sanke. Careful selection of broodstock, combined with vigorous culling, has brought about better skin quality, more vibrant colours, improved pattern definition and seemingly open-ended growth potential. Sanke have even been back-crossed to Magoi to gain extra show-winning length.

Koi breeders and suppliers

There is still no such thing as a 'typical' koi farmer; some of the best Kohaku continue to be produced part-time by a man with stock ponds in his suburban

Left: Koi-handling is an art. Here, a breeder moves a large Kohaku effortlessly from pond to bowl, for closer inspection by potential purchasers. Don't try this with your fish at home!

garage, while at the other end of the scale, Hiroji Sakai's koi farm in Hiroshima is a vast 'production line' facility. However, an infrastructure of breeders, wholesalers and shippers is in place to ensure that the international koi business is on a truly professional footing. Most breeders concentrate on one or two varieties, and all seek to achieve the ultimate accolade – Supreme Champion at the All-Japan Show.

Koi are now farmed worldwide, wherever the climate is suitable. Israel, the USA, China, Cyprus, Indonesia and South Africa are all major producers of koi for the volume market – which demands strong, healthy fish rather than perfect specimens – while Japan remains the homeland of top-quality koi. Major retailers visit the breeders routinely on buying trips, accompanied by hobbyists in search of their dream fish.

Making the most of the hobby

Modern koi-keepers have benefited from the mistakes of those who went before them. When koi first came to the West, it was thought that all they required was an unfiltered garden pond. Now we know that the hobby is really a science, and that koi need sophisticated filtration equipment and large, deep ponds to remain healthy. A vast support industry has duly grown up around koi – specialist dealers, manufacturers of equipment, professional pond builders and magazines devoted solely to these coloured carp.

Koi clubs and societies add the social element, while internet chatrooms are abuzz with discussions on the best cure for skin blemishes, the merits of wheatgerm pellets or the most economical way to heat a pond through the cold winter period. There has never been a better time to keep koi.

Buying and introducing koi

Imported koi undergo unavoidable stress and several changes of water as they are moved from breeder to holding station, and then embark on what can be a long, and perhaps delayed, flight. Arriving in their country of sale, there is more trauma while they travel by road or rail from the airport to the dealers and are introduced into their ponds. It is therefore essential that they are rested before you buy them.

Buying from a reliable dealer

Choosing a good dealer is even more important than deciding which fish you will take home. Your relationship should not begin and end with the sale of the koi. Ideally, you will be returning for advice, dry goods and more fish to build up your collection. You can tell a lot about a dealer from his premises; are they tidy and clean, are the ponds well-maintained, and do the koi look healthy and swim normally? As a beginner, it is always best to choose your dealer on recommendation and to take someone experienced along with you on your initial buying trips.

Buy only healthy-looking fish that behave and swim normally. This may seem obvious advice, but when an otherwise superb fish is marred only by a split fin, a raised scale or a small lesion, the temptation to buy can be strong, especially if the dealer reduces the price.

The value of quarantine

Before you consider a first purchase, set up a quarantine facility and ensure that your main pond is ready to receive koi. Home quarantine gives latent diseases or parasites a chance to manifest themselves. Most can be successfully treated in situ, while containing the problem. This is far better than compromising the safety of existing fish. However, there are untreatable viral infections around, such as koi herpes virus (KHV). With these, no matter how long you quarantine, you cannot be certain that your new fish are not carriers. This is another reason for choosing a reputable dealer who sources koi only from virus-free farms.

Home quarantine is only worthwhile if the water quality in your system is as good as that in the main pond, otherwise you may induce trouble rather than prevent it. Mix any new arrivals with one fish you have owned for some time, as this will show up any cross-infections, particularly with viral diseases.

Building up a koi collection

Buying koi should be a pleasurable experience, so set aside plenty of time. When you have seen a fish you like the look of, ask the vendor to 'bowl' it for you so that you can examine it at close quarters. Check for any damage, and if you are unhappy about any aspect of a koi, reject it.

Left: Your koi will be with you for a long time, so choose them carefully. View them in strong natural daylight, at close quarters, and don't be rushed or influenced by sales talk. The important thing is that you like what you are buying.

Your selection, once made, should be double-bagged in a little water with oxygen filling the space above, and packed in a light-proof outer box for the journey home. Place the box in the boot or rear passenger footwell of your car, drive smoothly and don't make unnecessary stops.

Once at your pond or quarantine vat, open the necks of the bags and roll them down to form a collar. Float the bags for no more than 20 minutes to equalise water temperature, then hold them open and allow the koi to swim free. Don't just tip them in. Net over the pond or quarantine facility for a couple of days – newly arrived koi are prone to jumping – and leave them in peace to adjust to their new surroundings. A couple of days without food will do them no harm. In a small quarantine vat, monitor water quality carefully, as koi that have been moved in transit bags can 'dump' toxic ammonia.

To support koi, your main pond must have a mature biological filter – one with enough beneficial bacteria to break down fish wastes that would otherwise quickly build up to toxic levels. You can buy filter start-up cultures, but there is no substitute for patience. Start with just a few koi, monitor water quality and perform regular diluting water changes until the filter bacteria are established. Only then should you add more fish. Your dealer will happily advise you on exactly what to do.

Tempting as it may be to buy many young koi and grow them on (thus saving money), fish under 25cm (10in) long are ill-equipped to survive their first winter in a temperate climate. Better to buy fewer, larger koi, which tend to be hardier. This, of course, does not apply if your pond is heated.

Stocking levels
Do not exceed recommended stocking levels (25cm/10in fish length per 454 litres/100 gallons maximum). Safe stocking density depends on the efficiency of your filtration, but as your aim is to grow koi at the optimum speed, it is not a good idea to fill the pond to maximum capacity. Add the fish gradually, so that the filter bacteria can keep pace with the steady rise in generated waste products.

Keeping koi healthy
There is no secret to keeping koi in good health – it is down to vigilance and common sense. Poor water quality is at the root of 90 percent of koi health problems, and water clarity alone is no indicator that it is safe for fish. Above all, fish require a stable environment, with a pH between 7.2 and 8.5, zero ammonia and nitrite, dissolved oxygen levels of 8ppm minimum, and nitrate below 25ppm. At the very least, you should routinely test for ammonia and nitrite, and use a pH meter. If you use chemical test kits, make sure that they are within their sell-by date, and if you use digital meters, keep them properly calibrated.

A heated pond is increasingly seen as obligatory, both to maintain an ambient temperature high enough to permit year-round feeding and to iron out

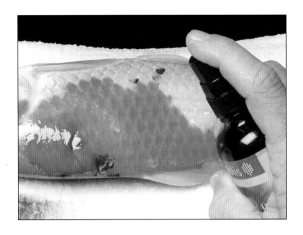

Above: Topical treatment of a wound with spray medication. With experience, minor problems with koi can be dealt with at home, but never be afraid to seek professional advice.

sudden fluctuations associated with unpredictable autumn and spring weather. Above 13°C (55°F), a koi's immune system will continue to function – below 10°C (50°F) it does not – and any temperature-sensitive medications you may need to administer will remain effective in warmer water.

Be vigilant
Finally, the best health insurance for koi is to look them over daily while they are feeding or swimming past. If a genuine problem arises, take immediate action. But don't always be netting out your fish for inspection without good cause. Netting brings about stress, however carefully done. If an otherwise healthy koi has a small, uninfected abrasion, and the water is warm and of good quality, it will usually heal itself without any intervention from you.

Left: It is human nature to want to build up a collection quickly, and see the different koi varieties interact in a 'living picture'. But patience early on will be rewarded by healthier fish in the longer term.

Feeding koi

Carp in natural ponds, lakes and rivers enjoy a self-renewing supply of aquatic insects, crustaceans and plant matter, which they get by grubbing through the silt. If there is not enough to go round, the fish do not starve, but instead of achieving their full growth potential, they remain stunted. On the other hand, a koi pond is a densely stocked, closed environment in which natural rules do not apply. The fish are dependent on their keeper for everything, including their food.

The koi diet

Nowadays, the trend has swung away from what the hobbyist could find in the grocery store or dig from the garden towards a heady selection of ready-prepared koi foods in flake, pelleted or extruded, pondstick formulae. While these are excellent, other foods given as treats to vary the monotony still have their place. Wholemeal bread in moderation, whole lettuce, oranges cut in half so that the koi can suck out the flesh, earthworms from chemical-free soil and even prawns in their shells definitely give the fish extra zest.

Avoid foods high in moisture and carbohydrate, such as peas, potatoes and sweetcorn. Twenty years ago these were koi staples, but only because nothing better was available. Also off the list are meat and dairy products, as these contain solid fats.

Koi do not have stomachs; digestion takes place in the long gut, and the more food that is offered at a sitting, the smaller the percentage assimilated. This is especially so at low temperatures. The remaining food is passed, partially digested, through the

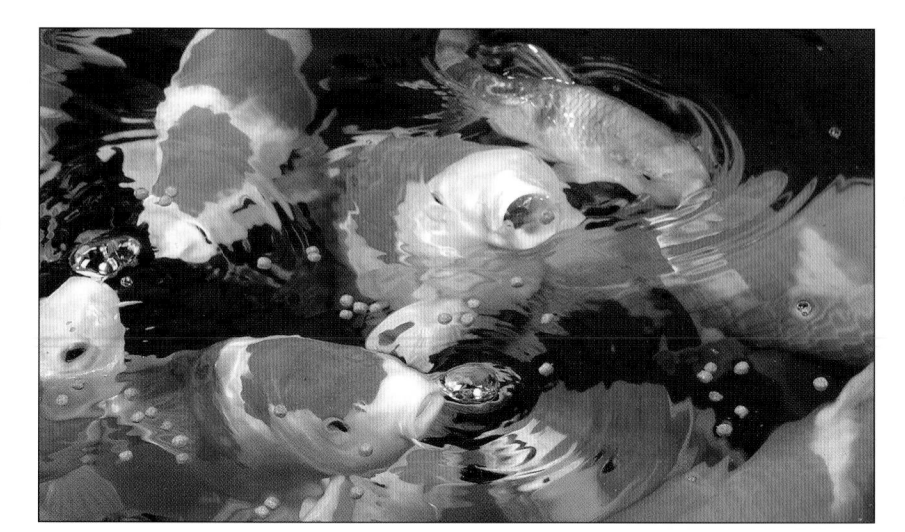

Left: Feeding time is when koi and their keepers interact the most. Koi always seem to be hungry, but unless you supply their rations on a 'little and often' basis they will not get the full nutritional benefit from their food, and you run the risk of overloading the filtration system.

digestive system to place an unwanted loading on the biofilter. Some of the least digestible ingredients in commercial foods happen to be cheap: carbohydrate accounts for between 30 and 40 percent by weight of a typical koi pellet and also acts as a binding and bulking agent.

This partially explains the great difference in price between similar-looking koi foods. High-protein formulae are more likely to contain fish meal, which provides desirable unsaturated lipids (oils). Other ingredients common to most foods are ash (a source of minerals), fibre (of doubtful value to koi), moisture and vitamins. Also present may be immune stimulants, probiotics (ingredients to pre-empt problems by nutritional, rather than chemical,

means), colour enhancers and various exotic additives, such as crushed crab and lobster shells, propolis – also known as 'bee glue' – and powdered montmorillonite clay. In a crowded marketplace, manufacturers are keen to gain the edge with innovative ingredients. The latest trend is towards paste foods in powder form, which can be mixed to a loose dough with water or fresh orange juice.

How and when to feed koi

Wild carp are constant browsers, but koi typically have to fit in with our busy work schedules and share our mealtimes two or three times a day. However, this gorge and starve régime does not promote the best growth rate. Invest in an auto-feeder, and the koi will come closer to nature with several, smaller meals over a 24-hour period.

In unheated ponds, what and how much you feed koi is temperature dependent. Start in spring, when the water reaches 10°C (50°F)-plus, with small amounts of easily digestible, sinking wheatgerm pellets. As the water warms further, move to higher-protein floating foods and then, when the pond begins to cool down again in autumn, revert to wheatgerm before ceasing feeding altogether. By then, the fishes' metabolism will have slowed and they will use their stored energy reserves through the winter. In heated ponds, koi can be grown on more quickly, with no checks, as they can be fed right through the year.

Few people bother to measure how much food they give their koi; the recommended amount is between one and two percent of body weight per day. However, young koi grow faster than large fish and require more protein. This is a case for not sticking with just one brand of food, but mixing several together for each feed. Remember that pellet size is dictated by the size of the smallest mouth in the pond – a yearling koi will not manage a 12mm (0.5in) diameter jumbo pellet.

Store all koi food in a cool, dry place in an airtight container, and never hold over any surplus from one season to the next. The vitamin content will oxidise, and there is the risk of harmful moulds developing.

Wholemeal or granary bread – feed sparingly.

The Vitamin C in fresh oranges is good for koi.

It is difficult to overfeed floating pondsticks, as they contain a lot of air. But koi soon become addicted!

Small-diameter pellets are essential when the pond contains mainly young koi.

Medium-sized pellets suit ponds with a range of koi of different sizes.

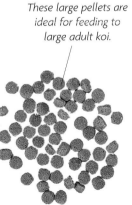

These large pellets are ideal for feeding to large adult koi.

Colour-enhancing spirulina pellets are thought by some koi-keepers to strengthen areas of red.

Above: *Once they get the hang of it, koi will enjoy nudging a whole lettuce around the pond and pulling off the leaves. Fresh green matter is beneficial to them.*

Breeding and showing koi

When koi hobbyists talk of breeding their koi, it is a very different affair from what goes on in Japan, or anywhere that these fish are produced commercially.

Flock spawnings

Flock, or uncontrolled, spawnings in koi ponds will occur spontaneously, provided sexually mature males and females are present, water temperature and light levels have been high enough and long enough ('degree days'), and there is a medium within which eggs can be laid and fertilised. However, many spawnings go unnoticed, because the parent koi immediately devour the eggs. Except in heavily planted ponds (or those with an unacceptably dense

Below: Flock spawning is a boisterous business. There is no control over which sperm joins with which egg, and surviving fry are unlikely to bear much resemblance to their parents, though there is always an outside chance.

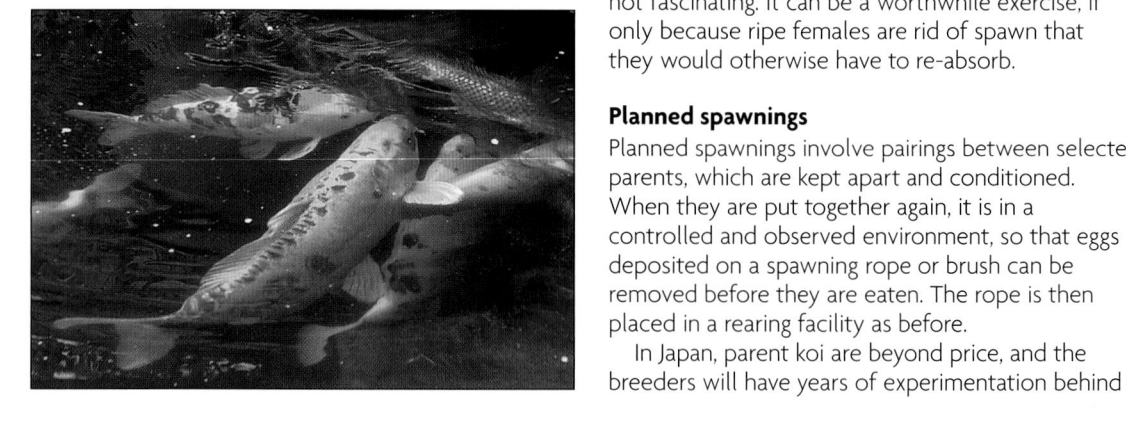

cover of blanketweed), any stray, free-swimming fry will soon be picked off. Brood survival depends on the koi-keeper intervening before the eggs hatch, separating them and then providing spacious accommodation and limitless live food as soon as the fry are able to take it.

The quality of flock-spawned 'home-breds' is generally very disappointing; the young fish display poor body shape and ill-defined patterns. The success rate is improved somewhat in the case of the less complex varieties: metallics crossed with metallics, or Chagoi with Chagoi. A few individuals will then develop into quite passable pondfish, though seldom reach show standard. Spawnings of Kohaku, Sanke and Showa are much more hit-and-miss, because there is no way of knowing their gene pool: handsome parents do not automatically produce good-looking progeny.

This is not to say that breeding your own koi is not fascinating. It can be a worthwhile exercise, if only because ripe females are rid of spawn that they would otherwise have to re-absorb.

Planned spawnings

Planned spawnings involve pairings between selected parents, which are kept apart and conditioned. When they are put together again, it is in a controlled and observed environment, so that eggs deposited on a spawning rope or brush can be removed before they are eaten. The rope is then placed in a rearing facility as before.

In Japan, parent koi are beyond price, and the breeders will have years of experimentation behind them, which gives them a good idea of which fish to put together to obtain the best results. Even so, massive fry cullings take place before even ordinary-grade fish emerge, and from an initial spawning, perhaps only a dozen koi will be true Tategoi (fine fish with scope for further improvement).

To rear koi through this scrupulous selection process requires pond space and funds unavailable to ordinary hobbyists. So, next time you complain about the price of a fish, it is worth remembering the work that went into producing it.

Showing koi

An obsession with showing koi is a quality shared by all top Japanese breeders and many hobbyists worldwide. To win the All-Japan Show is the dream of all serious koi producers, for emotional as well as financial reasons, while success at a hobby show confirms that fish are being kept properly and are reaching their full potential. Showing is also an opportunity to make a realistic comparison of your koi-keeping skills with those of others, and to meet like-minded people.

Aside from club shows, where entry is limited to members' koi, open shows tend to be held under the auspices of a governing body. In the USA it is the Associated Koi Clubs of America, in Japan and countries where there are affiliated chapters it is the ZNA (Zen Nippon Airinkai), while in the UK the British Koi Keepers Society (BKKS) holds sway. All these associations have 'apprentice' judges, trained to a uniformly high standard over many years before achieving full status.

What happens at a koi show

An open koi show follows one of two main formats. In one case, all koi of the same size and variety are exhibited in the same vat and moved around as the show progresses. In the second, each entrant has his or her own vats (holding facilities) in which the koi remain throughout the judging process. This option reduces the likelihood of disease transmission, but is more cumbersome to administer and harder for the judging team.

There are currently 13 judging classes and seven size categories in BKKS shows. A 'class', as this book reveals, may be single variety (e.g. Kohaku) or multiple variety (e.g. Hikarimoyo, which includes several types of metallic fish of more than one colour). The aim is always the same – to judge like against like fairly, culminating in the major awards of best baby, adult and mature koi. The overall supreme champion is chosen from these; in 99 percent of cases, this will be a large fish and either a Kohaku, a Sanke or a Showa.

Preparing for a show

To stand a good chance in open competition, you should first show your koi at club level. This will give some indication of their merit (and opinions may be at odds with those of their blinkered owner!). If the fish cross that hurdle, then to progress further in the show world, they need the right treatment if they are to look their best. As well as providing good basic pond husbandry and plenty of swimming space, feed them colour-enhancing foods as part of a varied diet. Heated ponds are vital to ensure that the koi attain a good size while they still have youthful skin, and of course, no koi should be entered into a show if it is in any way diseased, deformed, injured or carrying visible parasites.

Above: Part of the benching process involves measuring koi before they are entered into their size class (one of seven categories). This Showa will be held against the measuring scale to ensure fair play.

Right: Koi at a major Japanese show are transferred to their vats, where they will remain until judging is completed. The officials are well versed in the manual handling of large fish.

A responsible koi-owner will ensure that the fish arrive at a show in good condition, but once they are benched (sorted according to size and variety), responsibility for their welfare passes to the organisers. At the end of the show, when the koi are de-benched and returned to their owners, it is essential that all the facilities are there for a safe and stress-free journey home. It is up to the hobbyist to provide oxygen, plastic bags and transport boxes to ensure that this happens.

Many koi-keepers are not show minded, while others feel that the stress of moving fish around the country, however minimal, cannot be justified by the winning of rosettes and trophies. However, there is little doubt that the showing fraternity tends to own the best fish, and advances the hobby by pushing for ever-higher standards of koi and the means to keep them in the best conditions.

KOHAKU

Kohaku are white koi with red (hi) patterning. This deceptively simple, yet inspiring, combination makes them the most sought-after variety in the world. Many beginners are initially attracted by this minimalism, only to be lured away by more extravagantly arrayed, metallic fish. But the true connoisseur will come back to Kohaku with a heightened appreciation of the limitless interplay between two primary colours. No two Kohaku are alike, and that explains the fascination.

Patterns may be delicate and flowery (komoyo), or bold and imposing (omoyo). In either instance, quality Kohaku, particularly when large, convey the impression of quiet, graceful elegance, and rightly dominate the major awards in shows.

The Japanese have been breeding this variety for more than 100 years, over which time it has improved almost beyond recognition. It is one of only two types of koi (the other is Sanke) with traceable bloodlines, though pedigree is only one consideration among many when choosing Kohaku. At best it is a pointer, never a cast-iron guarantee, as to how a fish may develop. It is short-sighted to purchase only from breeders currently in the public eye – to do so is to miss out on some potential gems from lesser-known farms.

Three marks of a good Kohaku

The desirable elements in a top-class Kohaku are good body shape, skin quality and pattern. Of these, only skin quality is immediately apparent in young fish – beginners tend to confuse this with colour, which is quite another concept. 'Finished' hi (the

stable colour of an adult fish) should be a deep orange-red, but young Kohaku – even of the highest grade – that have not yet been given colour-enhancing food may look very insipid.

High-quality skin is difficult to describe, but unmistakable once seen. 'Lustre', 'depth', 'clarity' and 'purity' are all relevant attributes – good white skin carries a blemish-free sheen, as though the fish had been given several coats of silk emulsion paint.

Body shape changes as the koi grows. Young fish of both sexes are slim, but pointers to a Kohaku that

Below: In a young Kohaku such as this one, body potential is hard to assess. However, skin quality, pattern and depth of hi already mark out this koi as one to keep an eye on.

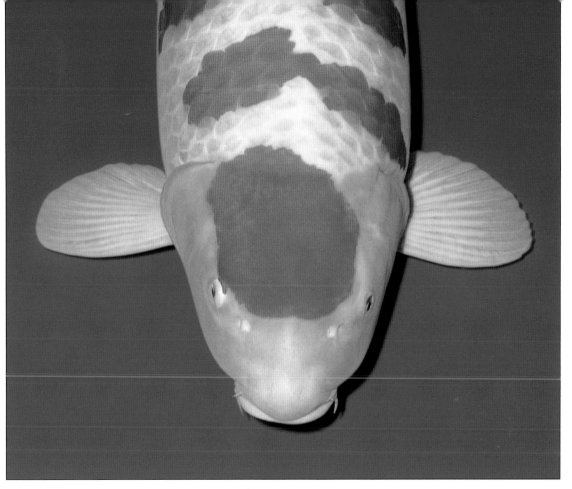

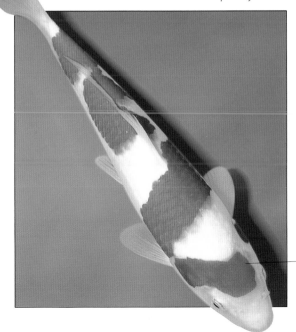

Opposing angles of head hi and the first pattern step highlight the pure white shoulders.

Above: One of the best koi in the world! This 90cm (36in) Maruten Kohaku was Grand Champion at the 2001 All-Japan Show. All elements are near perfect, especially the voluminous body shape.

will attain good volume in later life are a thick caudal peduncle (wrist of the tail) and broad shoulders. As to size, you cannot expect the koi to grow large unless it comes from large parent stock – this is where known bloodline comes into play.

Pattern, the third element, is what gives every Kohaku its unique character. The Japanese once laid down strict formal guidelines as to where the hi should be positioned on the white skin, and fish that fell outside these parameters were not highly valued. Today's attitude is far more relaxed, although the 'step' classification is still used for convenience – Nidan (two-step), Sandan (three-step), Yondan (four-step) and Godan (five-step). A 'step' is a stand-alone patch of hi anywhere on the head or body of the fish, but single, random red scales do not qualify.

All-important hi

Kohaku hi originates on the back of the fish and extends down over the flanks, as opposed to the 'wrapping' type of pattern seen in Showa, which can encircle the abdomen. When choosing Kohaku, it is important to understand that blocks of hi may 'break'. A young fish whose pattern resembles that of an accomplished adult may not have enough hi to see it through later life as its skin stretches, whereas a youngster with apparently over-heavy hi is more likely to 'grow into itself' as areas of hi separate away from one another.

Hi extending below the lateral line is not a fault, but it is better if it does not intrude into any of the fins. Ideally, in all Kohaku there should be an area of

Step-patterned Kohaku

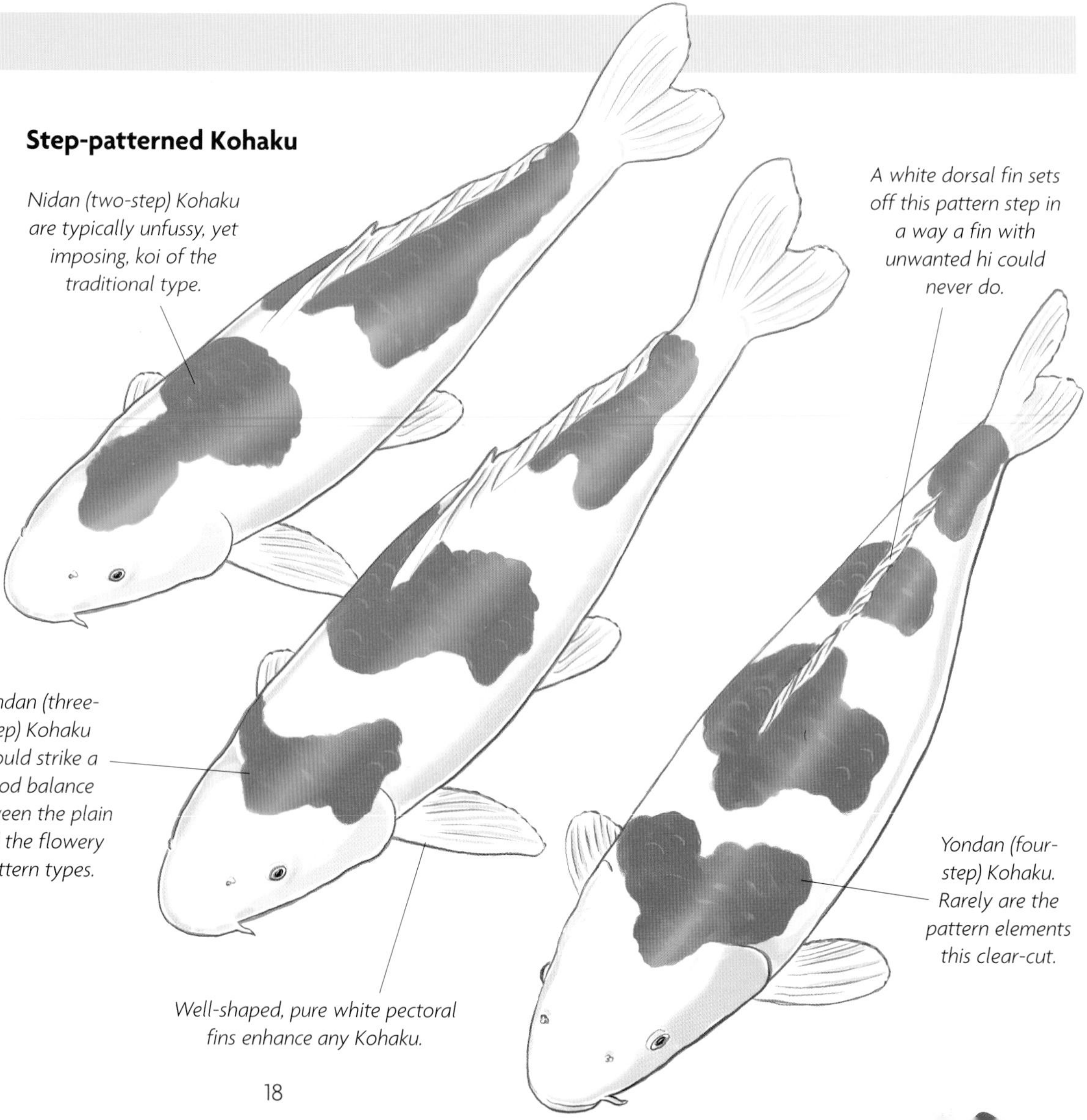

Nidan (two-step) Kohaku are typically unfussy, yet imposing, koi of the traditional type.

A white dorsal fin sets off this pattern step in a way a fin with unwanted hi could never do.

Sandan (three-step) Kohaku should strike a good balance between the plain and the flowery pattern types.

Yondan (four-step) Kohaku. Rarely are the pattern elements this clear-cut.

Well-shaped, pure white pectoral fins enhance any Kohaku.

Candidate for culling

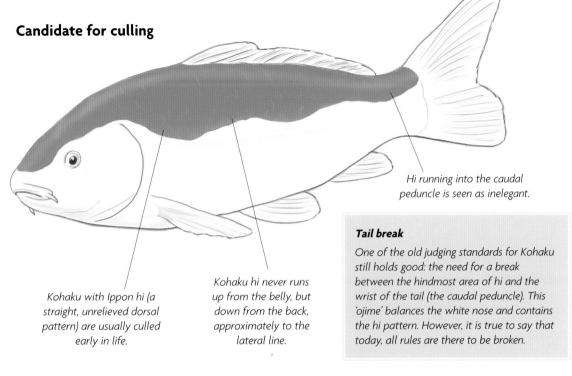

Kohaku with Ippon hi (a straight, unrelieved dorsal pattern) are usually culled early in life.

Kohaku hi never runs up from the belly, but down from the back, approximately to the lateral line.

Hi running into the caudal peduncle is seen as inelegant.

Tail break

One of the old judging standards for Kohaku still holds good: the need for a break between the hindmost area of hi and the wrist of the tail (the caudal peduncle). This 'ojime' balances the white nose and contains the hi pattern. However, it is true to say that today, all rules are there to be broken.

white separating the caudal peduncle from the hindmost hi step (ojime). But a tail region lacking any hi is a worse fault, as it unbalances the koi's overall appearance. Watch out, too, for pale and unstable secondary hi (nibani), a mark of poor quality fish, or pale 'windows', which may indicate that the Kohaku is in the process of losing its hi altogether.

Provided it forms an interesting pattern, unbroken hi running from the head towards the tail is quite acceptable. The best example is the Inazuma (lightning strike), where the red traces a more or less zigzag path across the back. However, Ippon hi (unrelieved hi all over the back and flanks) is not the

mark of a good Kohaku and fish like this are usually culled early in life. Other non-starters in Kohaku broods are Shiro Muji (all-white koi) and their opposite numbers, the all-red Aka Muji.

Head hi takes many forms. The ideal used to be a bold U-shape, centrally placed and extending level with the eyes, but never running into them. Now, though, the trend is towards Kohaku that 'break the rules' in a novel way. As long as the head pattern is interesting and complements the body hi, almost anything goes. In fact, fish like this tend to win shows because they stand out from the more traditionally patterned koi.

Above: This koi combines the zig-zag Inazuma (lightning strike) pattern with a Maruten head pattern and is therefore technically a Nidan (two-step) Kohaku.

Red lips are known as Kuchibeni (lipstick). They can counterpoint head hi that might otherwise seem uninteresting or sparse.

A fish with stand-alone head hi (quite separate from that on the body) is known as a Maruten Kohaku. This marking counts as a step pattern.

Hi is always more clear-cut on the scaleless head than elsewhere on the fish. Sashi (where white scales overlay hi at the front end of pattern) is never as clear-cut as kiwa (where red scales overlay white), but should be as sharp as possible. The hi of mature koi should be strong enough to disguise individual scales, but thin hi (kokesuke) will often deepen with age in Kohaku of good bloodline.

Lipstick lib

The Japanese used to be uneasy about Kuchibeni 'lipstick' markings on koi. They were a reminder of the heavy make-up used by Geisha girls, and therefore not respectable. However, in the West, such markings are seen as charming and cute, as well as serving to balance head patterns that stop well short of the koi's nose. Accordingly, breeders are meeting the demand for more koi of this type.

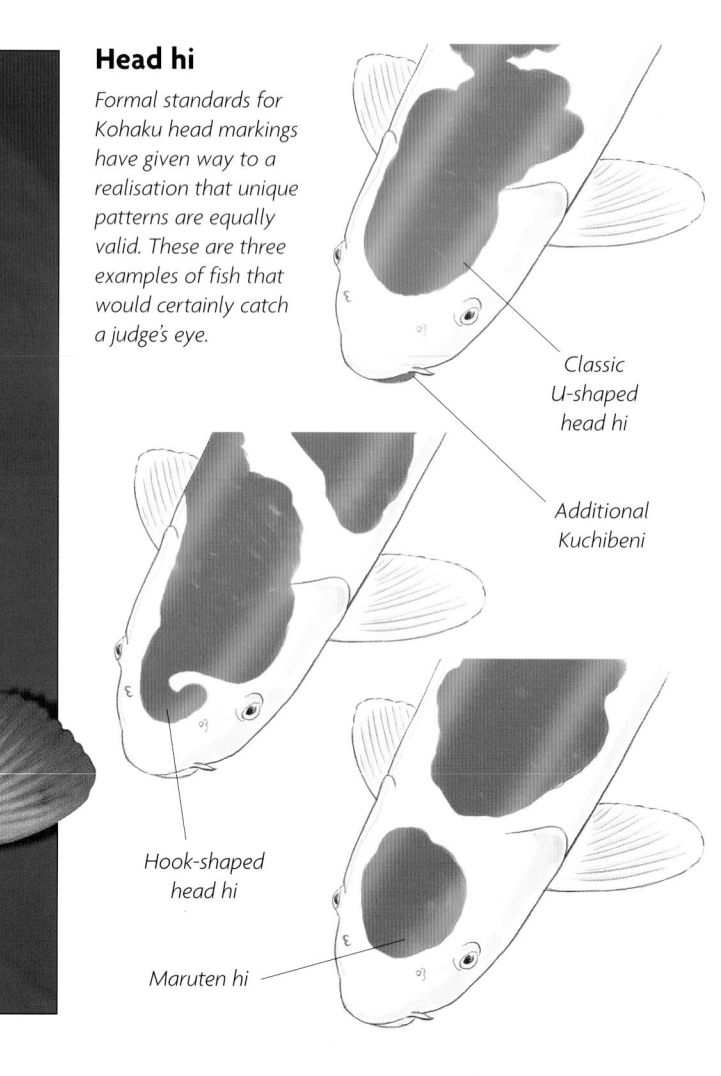

Right: *Clear-cut sashi (to the fore of each pattern step) combines with wonderful skin and body shape in a mature Yondan (four-step) Maruten Kohaku.*

Head hi

Formal standards for Kohaku head markings have given way to a realisation that unique patterns are equally valid. These are three examples of fish that would certainly catch a judge's eye.

Classic U-shaped head hi

Additional Kuchibeni

Hook-shaped head hi

Maruten hi

Doitsu, Gin-Rin, Metallic and other Kohaku

Doitsu Kohaku lack overall scaling. They make attractive, clear-cut pondfish, but in shows without a separate Doitsu class, all other attributes being equal, they will always lose out to fully scaled fish.

Gin-Rin Kohaku, with an abundance of reflective scales, join the other Go Sanke (Sanke and Showa) in their own judging class, Kin-Gin-Rin.

Metallic Kohaku (or Sakura Ogon) are judged in Hikarimoyo.

So-called 'Kanoko Kohaku' have dappled hi made up of clearly defined individual red scales. These fish often lose all their hi later in life, but where it is stable they are judged in Kawarimono.

Fore and aft

Because white scales always overlay red (sashi) to the fore of a pattern, Kohaku hi is never as clearly delineated here as it is to the rear (kiwa). As the hi thickens, the effect becomes less pronounced. It applies only to fully scaled koi, including Gin-Rin Kohaku and all other patterned varieties.

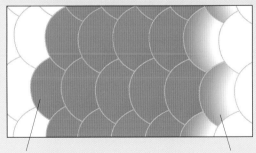

Kiwa, where red scales overlay white.

Sashi, where white scales overlay red.

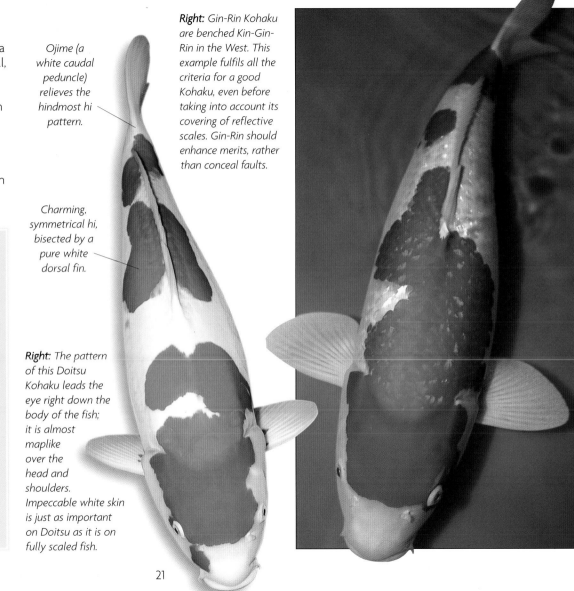

Ojime (a white caudal peduncle) relieves the hindmost hi pattern.

Charming, symmetrical hi, bisected by a pure white dorsal fin.

Right: Gin-Rin Kohaku are benched Kin-Gin-Rin in the West. This example fulfils all the criteria for a good Kohaku, even before taking into account its covering of reflective scales. Gin-Rin should enhance merits, rather than conceal faults.

Right: The pattern of this Doitsu Kohaku leads the eye right down the body of the fish; it is almost maplike over the head and shoulders. Impeccable white skin is just as important on Doitsu as it is on fully scaled fish.

21

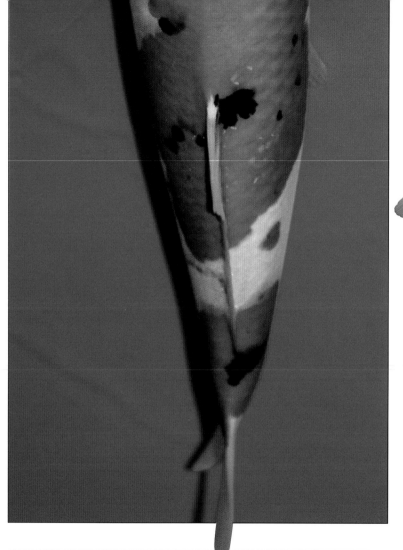

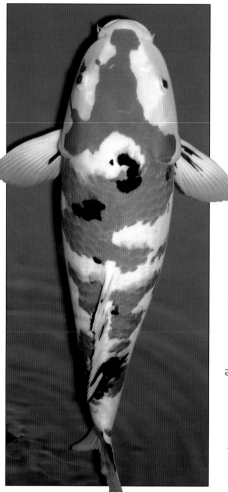

Sanke are koi that combine the red-on-white Kohaku pattern with the added element of sumi (black). When three, rather than two, colours interact there are many possible permutations — some bold and brash, others much more subtle. Hence Sanke work at all levels, appealing just as much to people who simply want attractive pondfish as to those whose aim is to win shows. As part of the Go Sanke triumvirate — the others being Kohaku and Showa — Sanke are highly esteemed in Japan, and no effort is being spared to refine and improve the variety.

The first Sanke

When recognisable Sanke first appeared is debatable, but tricoloured koi were probably around by the end of the nineteenth century. The old name 'Taisho Sanshoku' would place them in the period 1912-1926, and certainly the present-day bloodlines began when white fish with red and black markings appeared spontaneously in 1914 in a brood of Kohaku. Another breeder crossed the parent Kohaku with a Shiro Bekko (a white

Right: This Sanke has many unique features. Crown-shaped head hi, semicircular shoulder sumi and pleasing overall pattern are complemented by superb white skin.

koi with black Sanke-type markings), and one of the next-generation female offspring was run with a male Yagozen (bloodline name) Kohaku. The resulting Torazo bloodline, and an unrelated strain which has since died out, together form the genetic building blocks of Sanke today. Modern bloodlines include Jinbei, Sadazo, Kichinai and Matsunosuke.

Sanke patterns

Because Sanke are so closely linked with Kohaku, it is not surprising that the starting point for a good specimen is that it shows a credible Kohaku pattern. In other words, try to ignore the sumi and concentrate on the hi, which should be interestingly placed and strong in its own right. Although we do not speak of Nidan, Sandan or Yondan (step-patterned) Sanke, Kohaku-type block patterns are a feature of many of these koi. Sumi should not 'fill in' for deficiencies in hi distribution. The black is a complementary colour.

Choosing Sanke

Buying young high-grade Sanke can be exciting, not to say risky. Many of the best examples show little, if any, sumi until the age of two. Outwardly, they are Kohaku. Only the breeder can make an educated guess, from past experience, as to how these koi will develop, because the various bloodlines perform in very different ways. For example, Matsunosuke Sanke start life with very faint, blue-grey sumi that gradually deepens, whereas Kichinai Sanke appear 'finished' at an early age. Here, the only real change is that the skin stretches as it grows, affecting the distribution of hi and sumi over the white base colour. For that reason, young Sanke that are perfect miniatures of mature koi are not always a wise buy, although they may initially do well in shows.

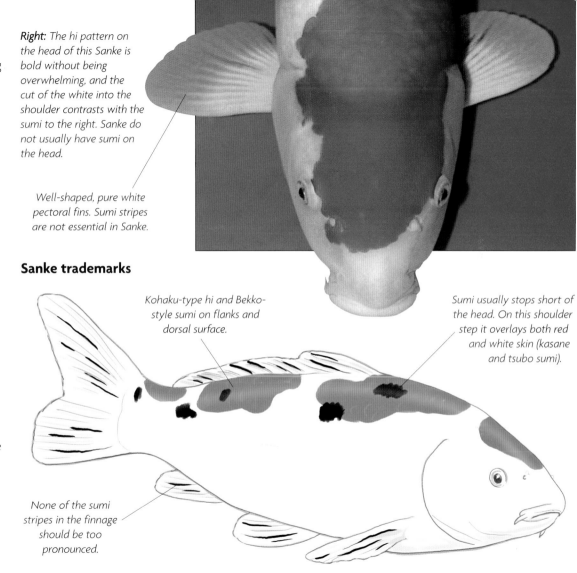

Right: The hi pattern on the head of this Sanke is bold without being overwhelming, and the cut of the white into the shoulder contrasts with the sumi to the right. Sanke do not usually have sumi on the head.

Well-shaped, pure white pectoral fins. Sumi stripes are not essential in Sanke.

Sanke trademarks

Kohaku-type hi and Bekko-style sumi on flanks and dorsal surface.

Sumi usually stops short of the head. On this shoulder step it overlays both red and white skin (kasane and tsubo sumi).

None of the sumi stripes in the finnage should be too pronounced.

SANKE

Sanke sumi in yearling koi may even vanish in the second season and reappear later. Early, stable sumi is called 'moto sumi', while black that appears later is known as 'ato sumi'. Sumi can overlay either hi (kasane sumi) or white skin (tsubo sumi). In most Sanke, both types are present, but those rare koi displaying only tsubo sumi are especially sought after. However, this situation may change, because tastes in Sanke are subject to fashion. Once, heavy sumi was in vogue. This gave way to a preference for minimalist sumi, present as strategically placed black accents. Now, almost anything goes, as long as the overall effect is pleasing. As with Kohaku, individuals that creatively break the rules and appear 'unique' tend to score over fish with more traditional patterns.

Certain ground rules, or Sanke 'trademarks', help distinguish them from the superficially similar Showa. Sanke sumi is of the Bekko, or tortoiseshell type, and rarely present below the lateral line or on the head. It may or may not extend into the finnage. If it does, the pectoral sumi typically takes the form of subtle stripes, rather than an aggregation of black in the ball joint area with stripes radiating from it – known in Showa as 'motoguro'. Nevertheless it is becoming ever harder to tell the two varieties apart, and no single 'trademark' can be a foolproof guide to identification. Only by evaluating them all together does the picture become clearer.

Sanke varieties

Tancho Sanke are effectively Shiro Bekko with additional hi confined to the head. These are benched Tancho. In Budo Sanke, all the hi is overlaid

Future champions

Tategoi Sanke are quality fish with potential to improve further. Hi may be thin, sumi sparse and body shape uninteresting, but good skin quality is non-negotiable; without it, the koi will never be more than a pretty pondfish. With Tategoi you buy a dream that may or may not become reality.

Above: *Pattern and skin quality already mark out this Tategoi Sanke as special. As more sumi emerges, the fish will become still more desirable.*

Revealing pecs

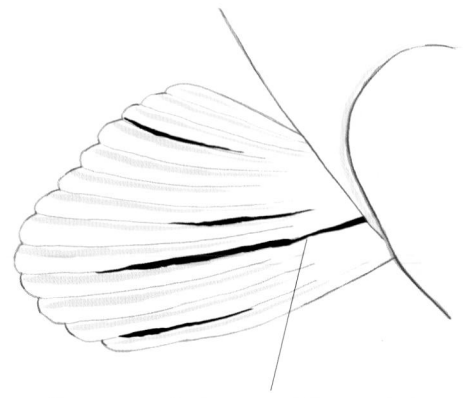

If present on Sanke pectoral fins, sumi takes the form of stripes.

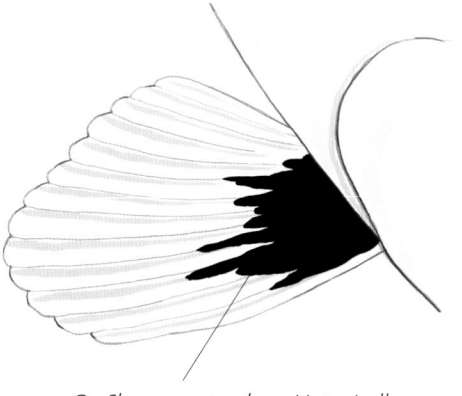

On Showa, pectoral sumi is typically concentrated in the ball joint of the fin (motoguro).

with sumi, to give a purplish effect. These fish are benched Kawarimono or Koromo. Otherwise, all matt-scaled Sanke are judged in their own class, and the terminology applied to them merely reflects the koi's appearance. For example, in Aka Sanke, hi is the dominant colour. Fish whose pattern runs unrelieved from head to tail, with no interesting white cut-ins, are not well thought of. Unsubtle as they are, good examples of Aka Sanke can still look very imposing.

Like their Kohaku counterparts, Maruten Sanke, have a patch of head hi not connected to the red markings on the body.

'Menkaburi' (meaning 'hood') is the term for head hi extending down over the nose and jaws, while Kuchibeni Sanke have the characteristic lipstick-like hi markings.

Gin-Rin Sanke display sparkling scales, too numerous to count; they appear gold over hi and silver over white skin. These koi are benched Gin-Rin, but can be confused with Sanke of the Matsunosuke bloodline, whose skin has a subtle shine termed 'fukurin'. There is an ongoing debate as to whether this term should apply to Go Sanke at all, but meanwhile these Matsunosuke fish continue to be benched Sanke, not Gin-Rin. A further refinement of Matsunosuke Sanke is that the bloodline has been back-crossed with ancestral Magoi to improve growth potential. Young fish, therefore, tend to be slimmer than most other koi, taking

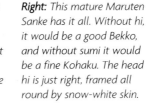

Below: A Doitsu Maruten Sanke with heavy, well-placed sumi. It could be mistaken for a Showa, but closer inspection reveals white, not black, to be the primary skin colour.

Right: This mature Maruten Sanke has it all. Without hi, it would be a good Bekko, and without sumi it would be a fine Kohaku. The head hi is just right, framed all round by snow-white skin.

several years to attain a voluminous body shape.

There is no identity crisis with Doitsu Sanke. These are very sharply dressed koi, with no scales to blur the pattern edges. Good examples look as though the colours have been applied thickly with a brush. In most Western shows they are benched with other Sanke, and fare poorly against them because they lack subtlety. However, in shows run along Japanese lines, they go into a separate Doitsu judging class, where they do not have to compete against fully scaled koi.

Metallic Sanke (Yamatonishiki) are benched Hikarimoyo, and all crosses between Sanke and other, non-metallic koi (except Koromo) go into the catch-all Kawarimono class.

SHOWA

Showa share an unlikely quality with polar bears — they both have black skin. In the bear this is hidden by thick white fur, while in the koi the sumi pigment may not always dominate. Nonetheless, Showa are always black fish with red and white markings. This distinguishes them from Sanke, which have white skin.

The first Showa

Of the three koi varieties collectively known as Go Sanke, Showa are by far the youngest. They can be traced back to 1927, when a breeder in Niigata crossed a Ki Utsuri (a black fish with yellow markings) with a Kohaku. As you might expect, this produced tricolour koi in which the hi was a washed-out orange. Only in 1965, when descendants of these early Showa were back-crossed to Sanke and other Kohaku, did proper scarlet hi and deep, glossy sumi begin to appear.

Showa do not have directly traceable bloodlines, and the continued introduction of Sanke genes is blurring the distinctions between the two varieties. The configuration, rather than the amount, of sumi remains the benchmark. In traditional Showa, where red is the predominant colour, the black takes the form of bold wrappings, sometimes extending up from the belly, and quite different to typical Sanke 'tortoiseshell' sumi of the Bekko type, which is confined to the area above the lateral line.

Showa signatures

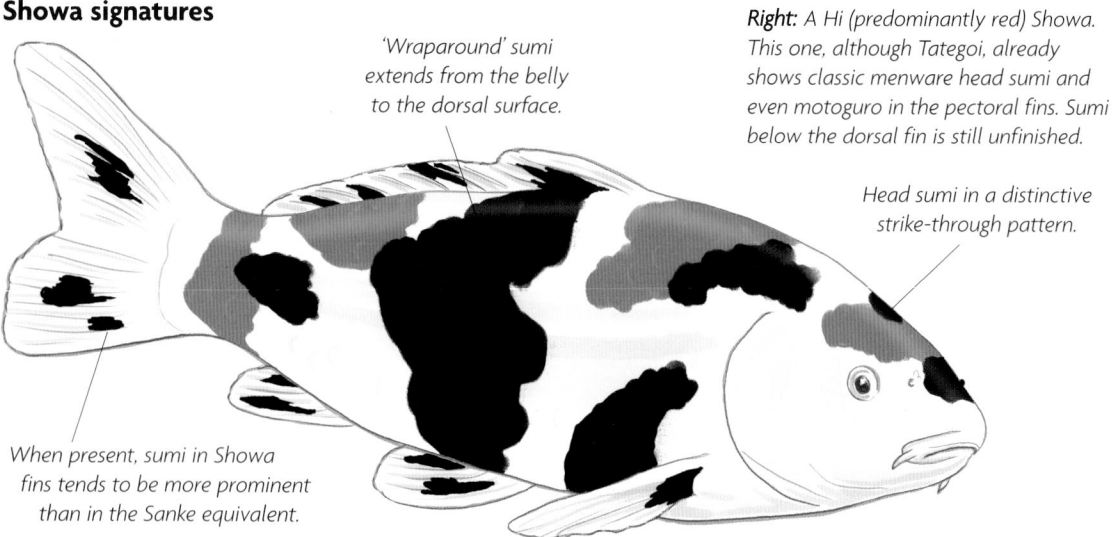

'Wraparound' sumi extends from the belly to the dorsal surface.

Head sumi in a distinctive strike-through pattern.

When present, sumi in Showa fins tends to be more prominent than in the Sanke equivalent.

Right: A Hi (predominantly red) Showa. This one, although Tategoi, already shows classic menware head sumi and even motoguro in the pectoral fins. Sumi below the dorsal fin is still unfinished.

Changing faces

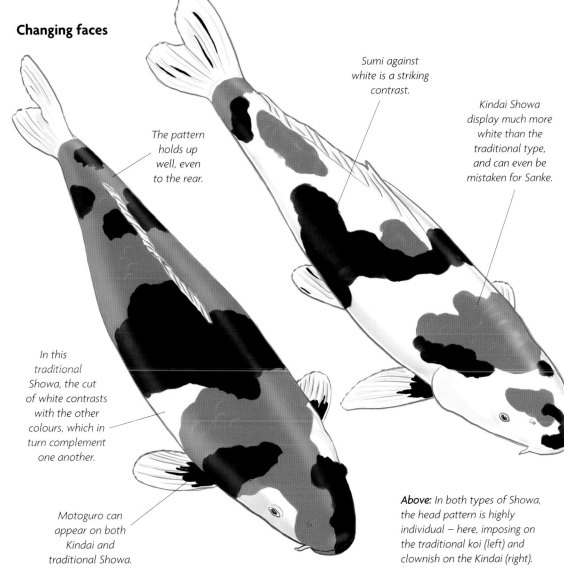

The pattern holds up well, even to the rear.

Sumi against white is a striking contrast.

Kindai Showa display much more white than the traditional type, and can even be mistaken for Sanke.

In this traditional Showa, the cut of white contrasts with the other colours, which in turn complement one another.

Motoguro can appear on both Kindai and traditional Showa.

Above: In both types of Showa, the head pattern is highly individual – here, imposing on the traditional koi (left) and clownish on the Kindai (right).

Showa patterns

Even on Kindai Showa – which, with their blinding white skin, seem at first glance to be more like Sanke – the sumi is the giveaway. It is nearly always present on the head, striking through the hi and white. 'Menware' sumi resembles a lightning bolt, while another well-known Showa head sumi configuration is V-shaped, starting on the shoulders, with the pointed end towards the nose. However, there is no set standard for Showa head markings. The important thing is that they are attractive: all-black heads, or smudged sumi, are not.

The Showa equivalent of an Aka Sanke is a Hi Showa (both 'aka' and 'hi' meaning red). But because Showa sumi is so bold and distinctive, it can lift the overall appearance of the koi, even when there is little white present. Hi Showa are easily confused with Hi Utsuri, which are black koi with exclusively red markings. If any white at all is visible on the body when the fish is viewed at a 45° angle, the koi is still Showa.

The ideal motoguro pattern on Showa pectoral fins consists of evenly matched semicircular blocks of sumi around the ball joints. These may be present in very young fish, or may develop through shrinkage of pigment in fins that start off all black. On the other hand, dark fins may remain that way. If they do, both left and right pectorals should mirror one another, otherwise the Showa will look unbalanced.

There is generally more sumi in Showa than in Sanke finnage although, again, some Kindai (predominantly white) Showa may show none at all.

Choosing Showa

More than any other koi variety, Showa are prone to physical deformities of the mouth and spine. If these are obvious, steer clear of the fish. More often, the defects are not that clear-cut and become apparent only on close inspection. View the koi from all angles, note how it swims, and give it a thorough looking over when it is first bagged up.

Another common failing is seen in Showa whose front-end patterning tails away to virtually nothing. Because the interaction of three colours is so successful, it is easy to be beguiled by a charming head, while failing to notice that the tail end of the fish lacks hi, or else is sumi-heavy.

Fully emerged Showa sumi should be a deep, glossy black, with no hint of chocolate brown. Hard water, rich in calcium and magnesium salts, brings out black better than soft water. Emergent sumi is

Below: *This Hi Showa shows both glossy black finished sumi and shadowy kage sumi just in front and to the side of the dorsal fin. Whether or not this fills in later, the fish has too much traditional sumi to be classed as a Kage Hi Showa.*

Right: *On this mature Showa, the kage sumi may by now be stabilised. As Kage Showa are not benched separately in the West, it is academic what this koi is called – opinions will vary.*

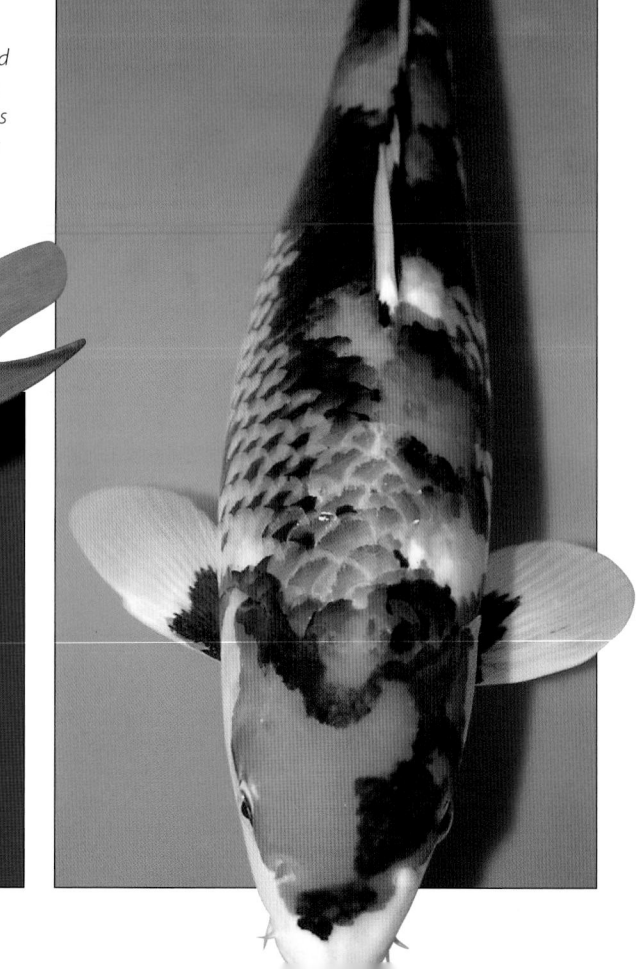

28

Left: A bright and beautiful Gin-Rin Kindai Showa. Tail-end sumi may yet become over-heavy, whereas that on the head still has some way to go. The striped pectoral fins merely enhance the overall effect.

Right: The saddle of white towards the tail of this Doitsu Showa, and more white on the head and shoulders, does not entirely relieve what some observers would regard as an oppressive pattern.

blue-grey, and forms a netlike pattern under the skin, which fills in with age. On some fish this dappled, shadowy sumi remains into adulthood, and the koi are then described as Kage Showa. In the West these were once benched Kawarimono, which led to disputes between owners and judges, because the distinction between finished and unfinished sumi is difficult to draw.

Showa varieties

No variety changes so radically with age as Showa. Babies can resemble Kohaku or Sanke, with only a hint of sumi. Hi markings, too, can come and go before they stabilise. This makes Showa a very exciting prospect, as even the breeders cannot tell with any certainty how pattern will develop. It may get better, it may get worse. So if you buy a young fish with good body shape and skin quality, its potential lies in the lap of the gods, to be maximised by good koi-keeping practice.

Tancho Showa are benched Tancho. Unlike in their Sanke counterparts, the head hi marking is usually struck through with sumi, rather than standing alone.

Gin-Rin Showa (benched Gin-Rin) are not very common in the West, but deserve to be: good examples practically glow. As in all Gin-Rin koi, the presence of sparkling scales should not blind you to obvious shortfalls in pattern or skin quality. Similarly, the white skin of Doitsu Showa must be the colour of snow, with no hint of a bluish tinge, and the enlarged scales along the dorsal surface and flanks need to be evenly arranged.

Some noteworthy Showa crosses include Koromo Showa, with interesting reticulation of the hi (benched Showa), and Showa Shusui (Doitsu fish where the dorsal scales are blue). These go into the Kawarimono class.

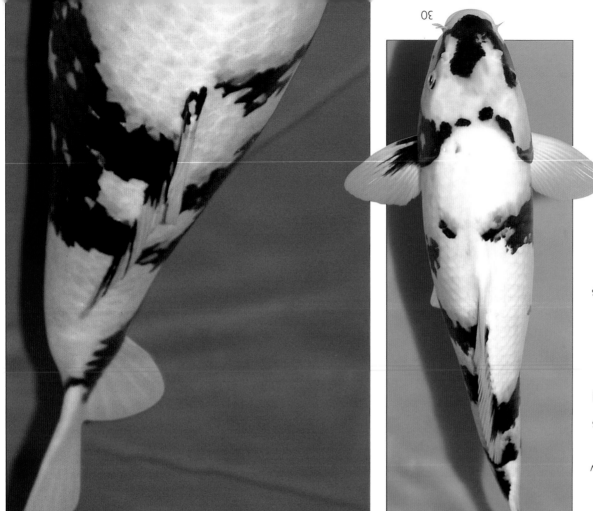

UTSURIMONO

The vagaries of fashion in koi-keeping are well demonstrated by changing tastes in black-and-white fish. Shiro Bekko — white koi with Sanke-style sumi — have fallen from public favour, if show entries are any yardstick, whereas the superficially similar Shiro Utsuri has achieved a status only a little below that of Kohaku, Sanke and Showa. This may be because the pattern is altogether bolder and, as a stand-alone feature, more interesting and variable than in Bekko, where the emphasis is on subtle understatement.

Shiro Utsuri are benched Utsurimono, a classification in which three varieties share the same type of sumi (black) — the primary skin colour. The others are Hi Utsuri (red on black) and Ki Utsuri (yellow on black). Although the latter was instrumental in the development of Showa, it is a variety seldom seen today, although its metallic equivalent, the Kin Ki Utsuri, is still common.

Shiro Utsuri are variously credited with direct Magoi antecedents or as being of more recent Showa descent. The sumi is certainly of the wraparound type, and in any Showa spawning there will always be fish lacking hi. Nowadays, however, Shiro Utsuri are so highly valued that 'accidental' examples are far outnumbered by fish bred from parents of that

Right: This Tategoi Shiro Utsuri already displays wonderful skin quality and sparse, though still-developing, sumi. Compare this with the mature fish pictured far right, which has a fully finished pattern and more voluminous body shape.

variety. As in Sanke and Kindai Showa, the preference for large amounts of sumi has given way to one for brighter fish in which the white predominates – although Shiro Utsuri of the original type are still valued, too.

Developing patterns

Looking at young fish, it is difficult to predict how the pattern will develop. Many of the best Tategoi Shiro Utsuri start life with only shadowy sumi markings that appear blue-grey under the skin. The best guideline is the koi's parentage, and whether fish from a given breeder tend towards light or heavy markings in adulthood.

Skin, too, can be deceptive in the early months, with a bluish tone and sometimes a yellowish tinge to the head, where there are no scales. This usually turns white as the skull bones and the skin covering them thicken. The wrist of the tail is where you will see the first indication of the final white ground colour and, all other things being equal, you should select the fish with the palest caudal peduncles. After that, it is down to part luck, part good water management. Hard, alkaline water brings out sumi to a finished deep, glossy black, although sumi of inferior Shiro Utsuri, on close inspection in good light, is more of a chocolate brown.

Head sumi, which may take years to emerge fully, is comparable to that of Showa, and may take either the traditional menware path or be more sparing and subtle. Excessively heavy head markings, or an over-fussy pattern on the face, will detract from the koi's appearance. Pattern symmetry is not important, but overall balance is. Too much, or not enough, sumi in the tail region is a common fault.

An otherwise excellent Shiro Utsuri can be ruined by its finnage. Some sumi is permitted on the dorsal,

Ideally, clear and motoguro pectoral fins should not be present on the same fish.

Right: *This head study of a Shiro Utsuri reveals the sumi to be of Showa type – wrapping around the body and travelling down the face as befits the primary skin colour. The white lips offer a pleasing counterpoint.*

Fin distinctions

Classic Shiro Utsuri pectoral fins show a sumi pattern known as 'motoguro', where the black forms a solid block around the ball joint. In Sanke, the equivalent pattern is made up of separated individual stripes following the fin rays. But as Sanke, Showa and Shiro Utsuri are interbred, intermediate pectoral sumi is becoming more common. All-black pectorals in Shiro Utsuri are a definite demerit, although the sumi may retreat as the fish matures.

Intermediate Shiro Utsuri sumi, where the black radiates outwards from the usual motoguro.

tail and undercarriage fins, but the pectorals should ideally resemble those of a Showa – either the classic matching motoguro markings around the ball joint or no sumi at all. All-black pectoral fins may later form motoguro; the worst pairing is black one side, white the other, especially if the fins do not contrast with the adjacent body colour.

Choosing Shiro Utsuri

Shiro Utsuri breed relatively true to variety, so good examples are far outnumbered by ordinary-grade fish whose body shape lets them down. When choosing from a number of youngsters, go for those with thick shoulders and caudal peduncle, refusing any that appear pinched-in behind the gill covers or have long, pointed heads.

In Gin-Rin Shiro Utsuri, the reflective scales show silver over both white skin and sumi, and the koi look very chic and not at all flashy. As with all Gin-Rin koi, the trick is to look beneath superficial finery and see if the fish stands up to scrutiny as a good representative of its variety. In the West, Gin-Rin Shiro Utsuri remain in the Utsurimono class, benched alongside conventionally scaled fish. To succeed against them they need to be not just good, but special.

Doitsu Shiro Utsuri could be confused with Kumonryu, and certainly the head markings are similar. Both are black-and-white, German-scaled fish, but Kumonryu patterning runs from head to tail, quite different from Utsuri-style wrapping.

Heads and shoulders

The classic menware (strike through) head pattern in a 'finished' fish.

This is an example of unconventional, but still attractive, divergent head sumi.

Here, separate V-shaped sumi patterns are balanced by a charming nose marking.

Hi Utsuri (black koi with red or orange markings) are essentially Showa minus the white and, as in Showa, the quality of the hi has been improved by outcrossings to Kohaku. There may even be Magoi genes present, to improve growth potential. Hi Utsuri pectoral fins rarely show motoguro, tending to be candy-striped black-and-red, with a red leading edge. It can be difficult to tell this variety from Hi Showa, but the latter always exhibit some white when viewed in the water, something Hi Utsuri never do.

Ki Utsuri, known until the early twentieth century as Kuro-Ki-Han, first appeared in 1875. The variety was stabilised and renamed by Eizaburo Hoshino, the same man who helped to develop modern Sanke bloodlines, but these days it is seldom seen. There are far more colourful yellow koi to choose from, without such a tendency to disfiguring 'shimis' – and buying a rare koi is no passport to show success, when it is unlikely that there will be others of its type present for comparison.

Right: One of the cleanest-cut koi possible is a Doitsu Shiro Utsuri. This one follows the modern trend of having predominantly white skin, although more sumi will probably emerge later, as this is still a young fish.

Left: A voluminous adult Hi Utsuri (a Showa minus the white). Dark pectorals are the norm for this variety, which should show minimal shimis, or black flecks, on the red ground.

An alternative name for koi is 'nishikigoi', meaning 'brocaded carp'. The pattern and scalation on some varieties does indeed form a rich tapestry, and to regard koi as living works of art is not to overstate the case.

The coming of Gin-Rin and metallic varieties has added new dimensions to this visual feast. Sometimes they enhance the overall effect. For example, a Gin-Rin Kohaku is none the worse for its coat of glittering scales – as long as the skin and pattern are of top quality. However, a metallic lustre may simply overcrowd and confuse the senses, and rather than improving the appearance of the koi may actually detract from it. This explains why metallic Ai Goromo (Shochikubai) and metallic Sanke (Yamatonishiki) are not as popular as the matt-scaled originals. Light passing through reflective pigment dulls the colours, making red appear orange and black more of a grey.

At the other end of the scale are koi varieties whose simplicity works against them. This is certainly true of the group benched Bekko. Although they retain their own classification, they are an ever-rarer presence at shows. Shiro Bekko (matt-scaled white koi with tortoiseshell sumi) are merely Sanke minus the hi. The best examples are chic and understated, but given the choice, most people would opt for Sanke, where a third colour presents so much more scope for individual excellence.

Before the production of Sanke (and Kindai Showa) with a high percentage of white skin, Shiro Bekko would be introduced to counterpoint other koi in a collection. Ponds in which one colour predominates never look as pleasing as those where fish are chosen, at least in part, for their contribution to the appearance of the group as a whole.

Shiro Bekko, still produced from parent fish of this variety, are just as likely to be thrown from Sanke spawnings. However, if there is any residual hi, they are merely inferior Sanke, and valueless for showing. Israeli-bred Bekko are on a par with those from Japan. They present a unique opportunity to own high-quality fish for a relatively low outlay.

Even ten years ago, acceptable Shiro Bekko sumi would be relatively heavy, in line with that of Sanke of the period.

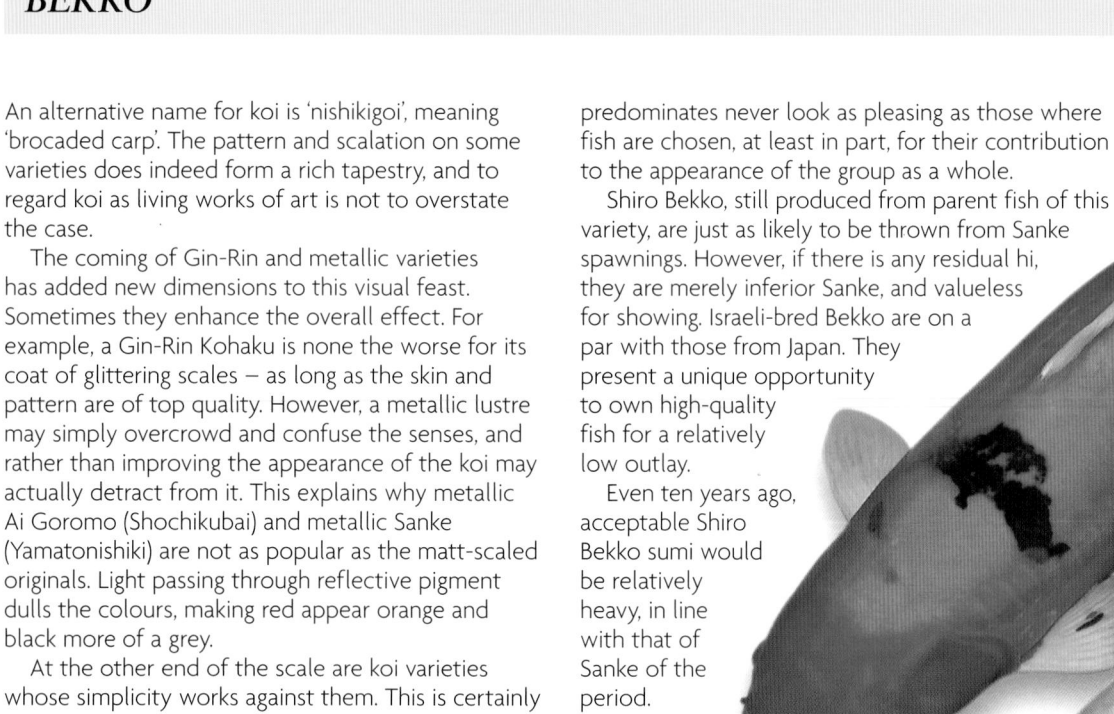

Both this Shiro Bekko and the Aka Bekko (above) have the desirable break between sumi and caudal peduncle.

Bekko sumi is always of Sanke, rather than Showa, type. This applies to finnage as well as to the body.

Above: *Clear heads are evident in both Aka (top) and Shiro Bekko. Looking at these examples, it is easy to see how both could be thrown from a Sanke spawning: one lacks the white, the other the hi, of a tricoloured fish.*

Despite a little white on the lips, this fish is an Aka Bekko rather than an Aka Sanke.

Nowadays, 'less is more'. The sumi, always confined to the area above the lateral line, can be extremely sparse, serving only to highlight a snow-white skin with a high lustre. A little sumi on the head is permissible, but the best examples still have a clear white face to show off their blue eyes. The heads of young Shiro Bekko are often yellowish, a colour that may fail to clear to white with age.

Sumi patterning should balance overall, and not be confined to one side of the fish. As in Kohaku, an area of white at the junction of body and tail fin is desirable – too much black at the rear end takes the eye in the wrong direction. Shiro Bekko pectoral finnage can be either clear white or striped with sumi, Sanke-style.

Aka Bekko are red koi with sumi markings – rare but striking. They are easily confused with Aka Sanke, which show a little white when viewed from above. The pectoral fins can be any combination of red and white, with or without sumi striping.

Ki Bekko (yellow fish with black markings) are the rarest in this group. Nowadays they are not deliberately spawned, but arise from Shiro Bekko x Kigoi or Sanke x Kigoi crosses. The commoner, metallic equivalent is the Toro (Tiger) Ogon.

Doitsu and Gin-Rin Shiro Bekko (both benched Bekko in the West) can be striking koi. The dorsal mirror scales of the Doitsu Bekko are silvery white, contrasting beautifully with any sumi they overlay, while Gin-Rin scalation enhances the subtle attributes of what can otherwise be an understated, and undervalued, variety.

Appealing blue eyes

Blue eyes are found in several varieties of koi, but look especially appealing in Bekko, offset by the clear white head.

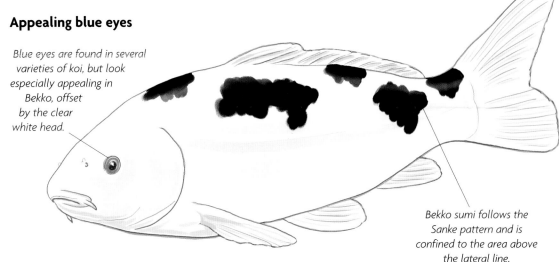

Bekko sumi follows the Sanke pattern and is confined to the area above the lateral line.

Asagi play a central role in the history of koi, as all other varieties have been developed from these fully scaled, non-metallic fish. How much interest they still generate can be judged only on present-day demand which, in the West at least, is on the decline.

Asagi closely resemble Asagi Magoi, of which there are two variants. The dark Konjo Asagi, bred as food fish, played a part in the development of Matsubagoi. Narumi Asagi, suitably refined, are the direct descendants of mutant fish named for their supposed resemblance to a blue fabric made in that town in Northern Japan. They had a blue reticulated back, and rusty red hi on the cheeks, flanks and pectoral fins. Leaving aside heightened colours and more evenly distributed hi, this description holds good for today's Asagi.

Ordinary-grade Asagi are easy to produce and uninspiring to look at, but nobody should dismiss this variety until they have seen a few prizewinning examples. The back should be evenly covered in pale blue scales with a darker outer edging. A sharp demarcation between the two shades produces the desired reticulation. With age, the skin stretches and this 'true fukurin' effect becomes yet more pronounced. The head should ideally be pure white, but is more likely to be grey or bluish, with spot blemishes

Hi Asagi and Taki Sanke

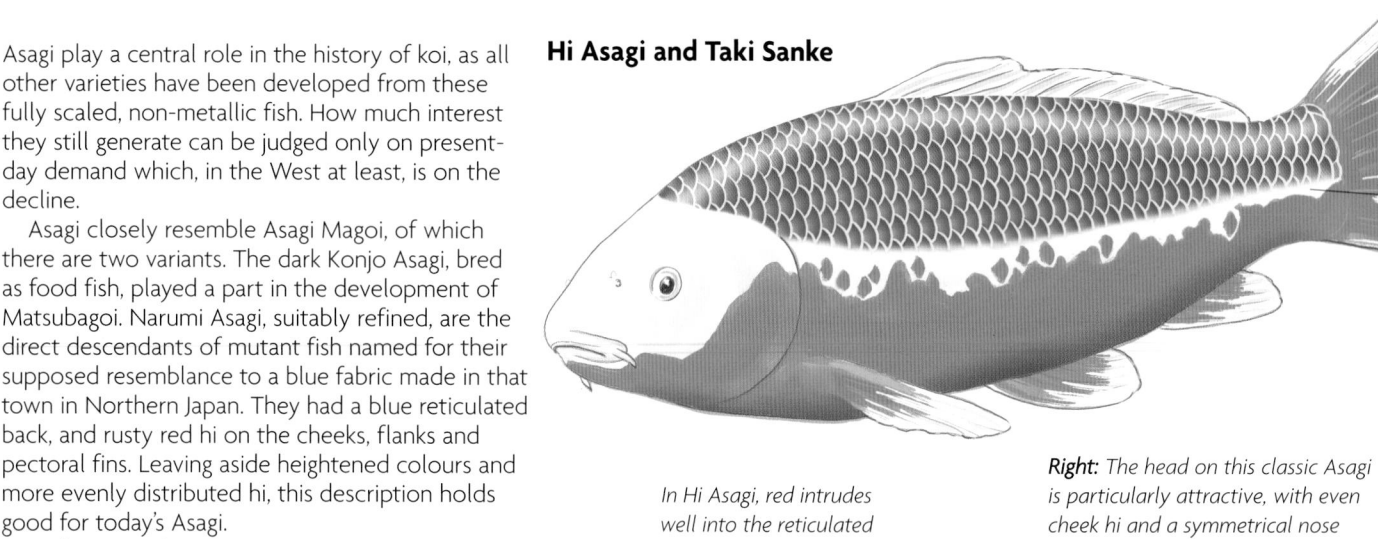

In Taki Sanke, a white flank stripe separates the blue back and red belly.

In Hi Asagi, red intrudes well into the reticulated blue ground colour.

Right: The head on this classic Asagi is particularly attractive, with even cheek hi and a symmetrical nose spot on an otherwise clear white ground. In fact, everything about this koi is balanced, even the pectoral finnage.

of hi. Larger hi markings on the jaw and cheeks are no fault, while if head hi forms a hoodlike pattern the fish is known as a Menkaburi Asagi.

On the body, hi runs up from the belly to the lateral line or beyond, although in low-grade Asagi hi can be absent altogether and the fish are a uniform blue. Pectoral fin hi is either configured like the motoguro of Showa or covers the fins entirely – the important thing is that it matches left and right.

Asagi with red markings reaching up almost to the dorsal surface are known as Hi Asagi. Taki Sanke (still Asagi, despite the name) have a white line separating areas of red and blue on the flanks.

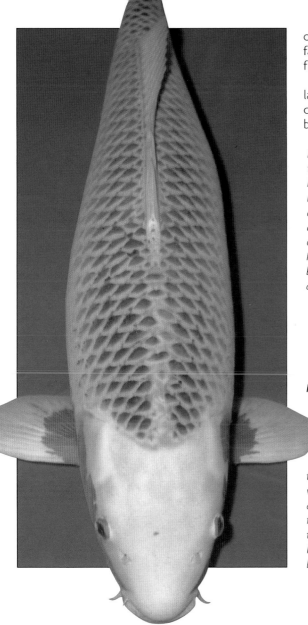

Left: This Asagi is hard to fault. The deep blue back shows even reticulation, the head is almost blemish-free, and the body is filled out without being fat. Note the demarcation between scaled body and scaleless head.

Hi over blue does not obscure the necessary scale reticulation.

Right: Hi and conventional Asagi demonstrate the variability of this very old koi variety. If the fish on the left were metallic, it would be a very acceptable Kujaku. In the fish to the right, blue is the dominant colour. Ideally, its head should be clearer than it is.

Shusui

Asagi belong in the same show classification as their Doitsu counterparts, Shusui – meaning 'Autumn water'. Shusui arose in about 1910 from crosses between Asagi and German carp with enlarged mirrorlike scales confined to the dorsal surface and lateral lines. This feature made them easier to clean for the table. Instead of a reticulated pattern, the smooth, sky-blue back is highlighted by this 'Doitsu' (German) scalation, which should form a regular pattern on the shoulders and run in two lines either side of the dorsal, reducing to a single line on the caudal peduncle. Other enlarged scales may follow the path of the lateral line.

On Hi Shusui, the red extends up over the back, complementing the dark blue Doitsu scales. Hana Shusui, too, have more red than normal, this time as an extra wavy-edged band between the lateral line and dorsal fin.

In Ki Shusui, yellow replaces the red. If the dorsal scales are black or greyish, this subvariety is easy to confuse with a Doitsu Ki Matsuba. (The greenish yellow Midorigoi, which is benched in Kawarimono, is also very Shusui-like.)

Shusui crosses include Showa Shusui, Sanke Shusui and Goshiki Shusui. These koi show characteristics of both parents, but with ice-blue, rather than white,

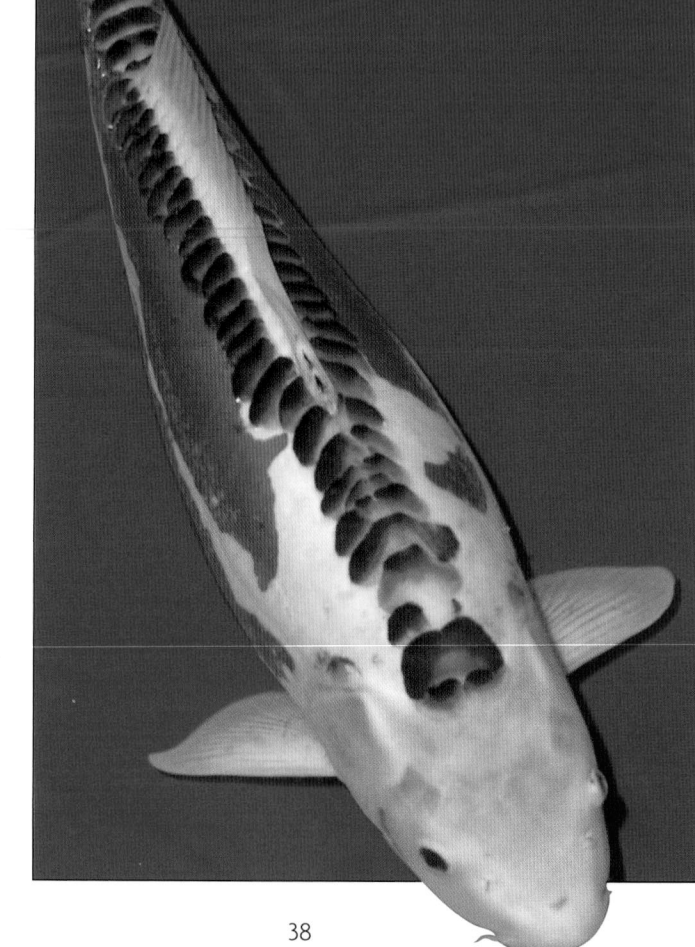

Right: The deep blue Doitsu scales on the dorsal surface of this Shusui set off both the bluish white and red areas of otherwise naked skin, but they could be more evenly aligned.

Above: Hi or Hana Shusui? It won't affect where this koi is judged, but in any event, red is a dominant colour on this attractive fish. Note the break between dorsal and shoulder scale patterns.

skin. They are benched Kawarimono. Shusui crossed with metallic Ogons result in Ginsui and Kinsui, which are rarely seen today.

When choosing Shusui, watch out for messy or asymmetrical shoulder scale patterns, or individual rogue scales appearing anywhere on the body – particularly the belly. A clear head is an essential requisite. In hard water, the mirror scales can turn greyish or black, and once this happens they never revert back to blue. Shusui are also prone to shimis and middle-aged spread, so to grow on a fish that retains a good shape and clear colours is quite an achievement.

Right: This idealised example of a Shusui shows a perfectly symmetrical pattern and Doitsu scalation rarely encountered in the flesh. The whiter the head, the better – in practice, it tends more towards the ice-blue of the body.

An otherwise excellent Shusui can be ruined by unbalanced pectoral fin markings.

Hi Shusui and Ki Shusui

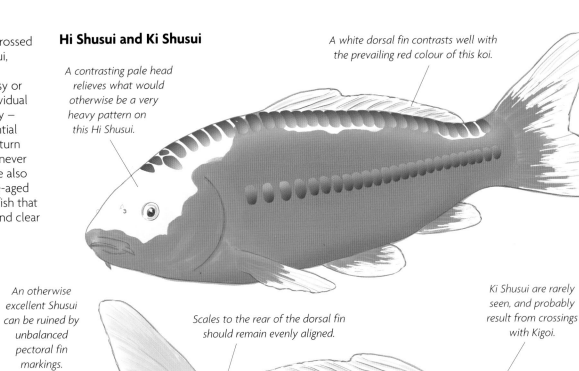

A contrasting pale head relieves what would otherwise be a very heavy pattern on this Hi Shusui.

A white dorsal fin contrasts well with the prevailing red colour of this koi.

Scales to the rear of the dorsal fin should remain evenly aligned.

Ki Shusui are rarely seen, and probably result from crossings with Kigoi.

In this Ki Shusui, yellow largely replaces hi.

39

KOROMO

Koromo are cross-bred koi (hybridisation is another matter, involving parents of different species). Most koi varieties stem from crossings, but in Koromo the parentage is very obvious – Kohaku and Asagi. Koromo is the Japanese word for 'robed', and aptly describes a group of koi that first became available in the 1950s. From the Kohaku side of the family tree comes white skin with a hi pattern, while the Asagi genes contribute black or blue secondary colours to the red areas alone. In the West the issue is no longer quite so clear-cut, as Goshiki (five-colour koi) are now included in Koromo. In these koi, the pattern overlay intrudes into the white skin. The change in classification was made to avoid show benching disputes in borderline cases.

The classic Koromo is the Ai Goromo, and a good example should display all the qualities expected of a Kohaku – snow-white skin and deep crimson hi. Blue or blue-black scale reticulation may take years to emerge fully over the hi. Whether it then confines itself to these areas, or moves further over the body, determines whether the fish remains an Ai Goromo or becomes a Goshiki. Some individuals are legitimately benched in both varieties at different stages in their lives.

Young high-quality Ai Goromo can appear very Kohaku-like, which is no bad thing. A robed pattern that emerges too early may develop to

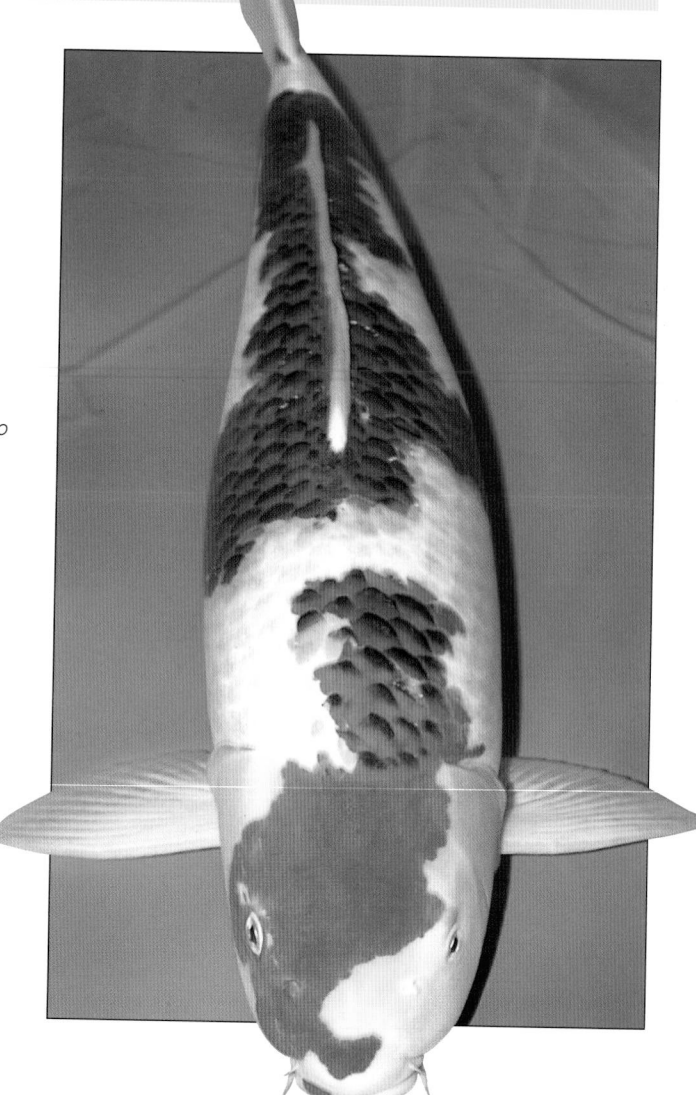

An Ai Goromo needs a good Kohaku pattern as the base for its 'robing' of blue over hi.

Right: *A mature Ai Goromo with well-defined scale reticulation. In this variety the head can be either plain or patterned – this fish has particularly interesting hi running down the face.*

Left: *Young Ai Goromo can look very much like Kohaku for up to three years. This Tategoi has yet to develop full robing, but all the other elements are in place, including superb skin and an interesting Inazuma (lightning strike) pattern.*

excess and overwhelm the koi. In mature fish the blue scale centres should be evenly distributed over all patches of hi, with the exception of any present on the head.

Sumi Goromo are white koi with a black pattern, each scale of which is edged in red – a mirror image of what happens in Ai Goromo. Very occasionally, none of this red edging emerges, and we are left with a 'black Kohaku' which would have to be benched Kawarimono.

Another definition of a Sumi Goromo is a red-and-white koi in which all areas of hi, including those on the head, are fully overlaid with black. These fish have a quiet elegance but, in truth, dark Ai Goromo and light Sumi Goromo can look very similar.

A Budo Goromo is a Sumi Goromo variant with purplish patches of overlaid hi. Kiwa and sashi show as individual scales picked out against the white, reminiscent of bunches of grapes in shape and colour. The very similar Budo Sanke has sumi overlaying the hi, with additional solid Sanke-type 'Hon' sumi markings. The inference to draw is that they result from Sumi Goromo/Sanke crosses.

Left: *In Budo Goromo, the form the pattern takes defines the variety just as much as its colours; the combined elements are said to resemble bunches of grapes. The pure white head on this koi offers a startling contrast.*

Right: *A mature three-step Sumi Goromo has an almost maplike pattern around the dorsal fin. Scale reticulation is less pronounced than on an Ai Goromo, as sumi fully overlays the hi.*

KOROMO

Doitsu Ai Goromo are among the rarest of koi. The only blue/black scales are the enlarged ones running along the back. In all other respects the fish is a Doitsu Kohaku, with no intrusion of another colour into the body hi. In the West, all Doitsugoi, with the exception of Go Sanke, are benched under their own variety, so the correct classification of this type of fish is Koromo.

Goshiki, the 'new recruits' to Koromo, are allegedly five-coloured koi – red, black, white, and light and dark blue. The traditional Goshiki is a dark fish with rather indistinct patterning, sometimes relieved by clear patches of hi. Others look like straight Kohaku x Asagi crosses, with a black reticulation over the whole body. A sixth colour, purple, is apparent when sumi overlays blue. Modern Goshiki closely resemble Koromo Showa. By no means all the hi is overlaid,

Something for everyone

Within the Goshiki variety are fish so diverse in appearance that beginners to koi-keeping would never dream they are grouped together. At one extreme are dark, rather muddy-looking koi; at the other, fish with superb pattern definition, plenty of clear white skin and real 'presence'. Modern Goshiki are right up among Go Sanke in terms of koi that can be appreciated at several levels, and the best examples command high prices.

Above: *This Goshiki is also Gin-Rin, but the sparkling scales only show to good effect because the overall pattern is so good – even though the fish lacks much white. Pectoral fin hi harks back to Asagi lineage.*

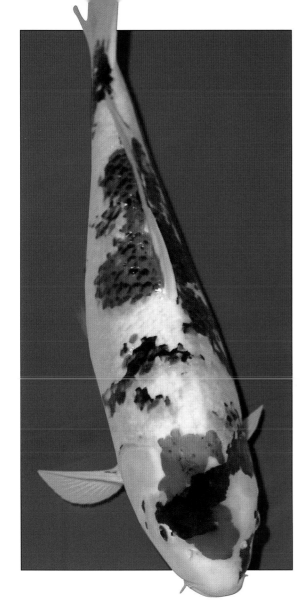

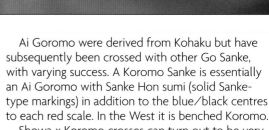

Right: At the time of writing, this is far and away the best Goshiki in the UK. The reticulated and scalloped hi pattern stands out against milk-white skin, and the head, with blue eyes and a charming nose spot, is beguiling.

Left: For quiet sophistication, a good Koromo Showa is hard to beat. The scale reticulation on this example is confined to the body hi, contrasting with the oblique mask of solid face sumi of Showa derivation.

and sometimes fish show reticulation only over the secondary colours. They can be confused at first glance with Kujaku, but these are metallic, not matt, koi. White is the prevailing colour in modern Goshiki, giving these fish a clear-cut look.

In Gin-Rin Goshiki, where the appearance of the reflective scales is determined by the skin tones beneath, almost limitless colour permutations are possible. Doitsu Goshiki, by contrast, are quite subdued. The blue from the Asagi lineage cannot form a reticulated pattern, as there are no scales: instead, blocks of subtle colour characterise these somewhat uncommon fish.

Ai Goromo were derived from Kohaku but have subsequently been crossed with other Go Sanke, with varying success. A Koromo Sanke is essentially an Ai Goromo with Sanke Hon sumi (solid Sanke-type markings) in addition to the blue/black centres to each red scale. In the West it is benched Koromo.

Showa x Koromo crosses can turn out to be very sophisticated-looking koi. The fact that the hi tends to be brownish red, rather than crimson, does not matter. It serves as a subtle ground colour over which the Hon sumi runs, extending over the head in typical Showa fashion. But all Koromo, these included, must have impeccable white skin.

KAWARIMONO

Koi benched Kawarimono are non-metallic fish of named varieties that do not fall within other classifications. This diverse group takes in Doitsu (scaleless) and Gin-Rin (koi with reflective silver scales), as well as fully-scaled matt koi, of one or more colours, and includes fish of the Karasu lineage, which are close to the ancestral Magoi.

Also placed in Kawarimono are the true 'one-offs', or unique koi – pleasing, non-metallic crosses whose exact parentage may or may not be apparent.

The Kawarimono class is well represented at shows, due in large measure to the popularity of Chagoi and Kumonryu. Within the group are fish to appeal to all hobbyists, and few ponds are without some representatives.

Single-coloured koi

All-red Kohaku are usually culled early in the selection process, but if the hi is of exceptional quality the fish may be grown on as a saleable commodity. They are known as Benigoi or Aka Muji. In such plain koi, good body shape and blemish-free skin are paramount. If a Benigoi has white tips to the finnage, it becomes an Aka Hajiro.

Also thrown up in Kohaku broods are all-white koi called Shiro Muji. Their plain appearance goes against most tastes, but

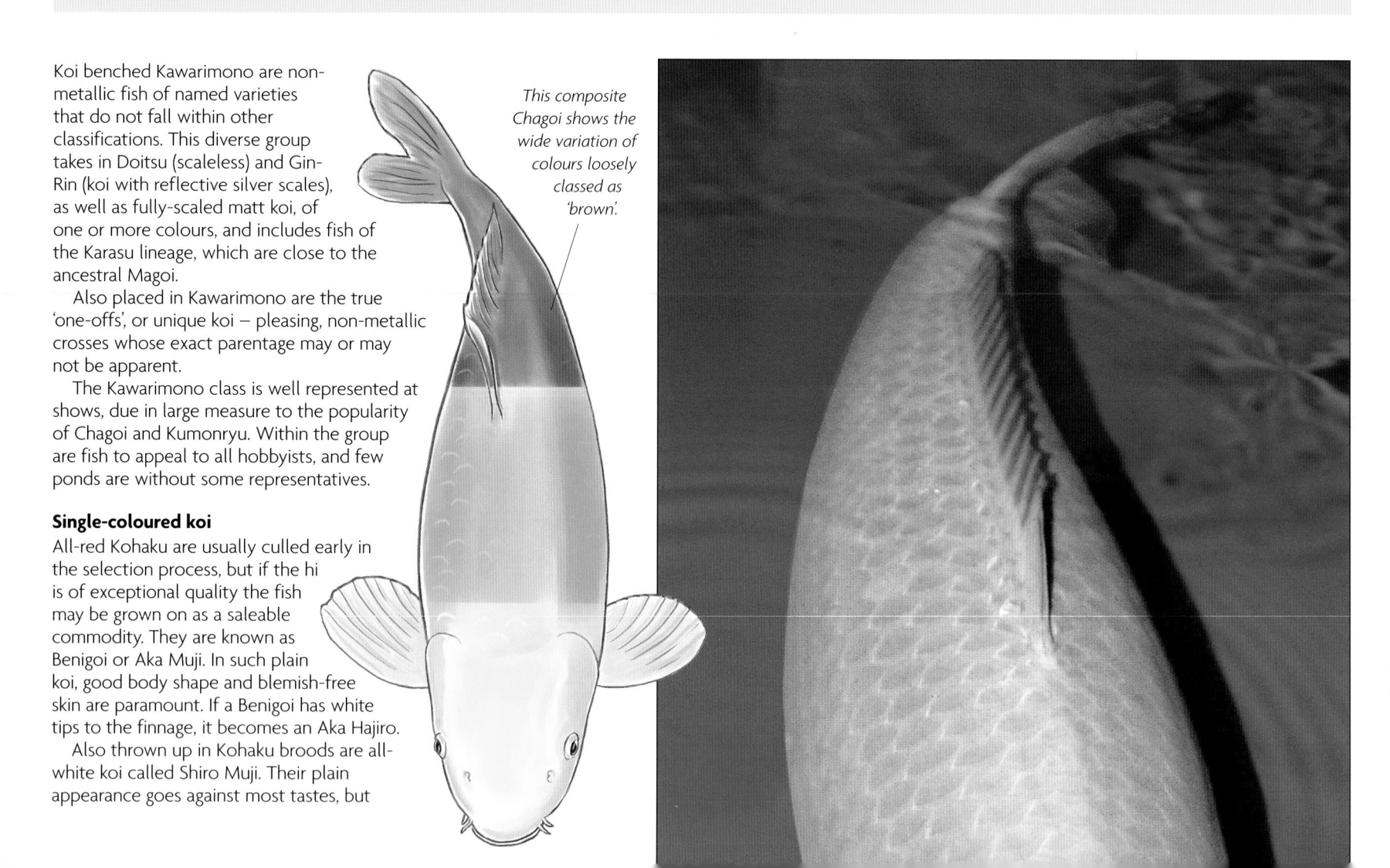

This composite Chagoi shows the wide variation of colours loosely classed as 'brown'.

Left: In this Gin-Rin Chagoi, the uniform base colour is lifted by a full coat of sparkling scales. Imagine what this koi will look like when it attains 90cm (36in) or more, which Chagoi frequently do.

Right: A large, saffron-coloured Chagoi is typically the 'character' fish in a pond, acting as a soothing influence on younger, more skittish fish. However, Chagoi are greedy and often grow fat.

a large example with flawless skin is a sight to behold. There is also a rare red-eyed (albino) variant, which is highly prized.

Kigoi (yellow koi) are a very old variety, enjoying something of a comeback. Males, in particular, can attain lengths of 90cm (36in) or more, though usually not with proportionate volume. The colour (the deeper the better) should be uniform across the back and flanks, shading to a silvery belly. Black-eyed Kigoi are the most commonly available, but the red-eyed (Akame) fish command a higher price.

Magoi are the koi that started it all – the so-called 'black carp' from which all other varieties were subsequently developed. In fact, their colour is a deep bronze, rather than a velvety black. They are strong, vigorous fish and can grow huge. Most show organisers will not accept Magoi as a true koi variety, but large, scale-perfect examples are bred in Japan and find a ready market as pieces of living history.

Chagoi (tea-coloured koi), plain or Gin-Rin, are bred in shades from pale buff to almost brick red. Fully-scaled examples need to display well-defined reticulation, while in Doitsu fish the enlarged scales along the lateral line and the two lines running either side of the dorsal fin should be neat and even. These are the giants among the true koi varieties, and in a heated pond can attain 90cm (36in) in just five or six years. Their understated appearance is a good foil to more colourful koi, but their real appeal is their extreme friendliness; they quickly become hand-tame, which encourages their pondmates to follow suit. Mass-production of Chagoi means that good examples are becoming harder to find; also beware of metallic finnage which, although attractive, precludes fish from inclusion in Kawarimono.

The blue-grey Soragoi share the growth potential and friendly disposition of Chagoi.

Few Doitsu koi are assigned to a variety on the basis of their German-type scalation, but in Kawarimono we find two – one being Kumonryu (see page 47), the other Midorigoi. Midorigoi are said to be green, although as they grow, 'greenish yellow' is a more accurate description. They have an almost translucent quality, as though lit from within, and bear a superficial resemblance to poor-quality Doitsu Kin Matsuba (metallic gold koi with pinecone scalation). However, the skin of Midorigoi is always non-metallic.

Matsubagoi (fish displaying 'pinecone' scalation) are mostly grouped in Hikarimuji, the classification for single-coloured metallic koi, even though to Western eyes the dark edging to the scales constitutes a second colour. However, one or two non-metallic varieties belong in Kawarimono.

Aka Matsuba could be described as Asagi (see page 36) lacking any blue. The ground colour is red, each dorsal and flank scale being edged in black. In Ki Matsuba the primary colour is yellow and in Shiro Matsuba it is white.

Kawarimono of more than one colour

Ochibashigure (usually abbreviated to 'Ochiba') result from crosses between Chagoi and Soragoi. Grey is the ground colour, the brown in the best examples forming a Kohaku-like pattern. However,

Right: The only 'green' koi you are likely to see is a Midorigoi. They are always Doitsu. This one has the typical translucent skin associated with the variety, and particularly well-aligned scales.

Left: An Ochibashigure with almost Kohaku-like patterning, resulting from a Chagoi x Soragoi cross. Good scale reticulation is essential in this relatively new variety. Brown on grey is a highly subtle colour combination.

Netlike scale edging defines the pattern of an Ochiba.

Unique koi

'One-off' koi, difficult to assign to any single variety or recognisable cross, can be benched Kawarimono as long as they are matt-scaled. Many home-breds fall into this category, but whatever their ancestry, they will never make the grade without good body shape and skin quality. These attributes rarely occur in koi from random, flock spawnings.

fish for the mass market tend to lean heavily towards one or the other element, and could be more accurately described as Chagoi with some grey, or Soragoi with a little brown. Well-defined scale reticulation in non-Doitsu examples is a must.

'Kanoko' means 'dappled'. Instead of having solid hi, some Kohaku, Sanke and Showa exhibit clusters of individually defined red scales, which may or may not be an early sign that the hi is breaking up and disappearing. If it remains, these Kanoko fish are benched Kawarimono, rather than under their own varieties, as clearly they would not be able to compete on equal terms with more conventionally patterned examples.

Kawarimono of Karasu lineage

A Karasu, or Karasugoi (meaning 'crow'), is superficially similar to a Magoi, but the body is a deep, velvety black and the belly can be white, red or orange. Doitsu and fully-scaled fish are recognised. From the Karasu have arisen other koi with varying degrees of white on the fins and/or body, and these are named varieties. A Hajiro has a white-tipped nose, tail, dorsal and pectoral fins, which all serve to accent the black body. In Hageshiro, the white extends to the whole head, while a Yotsujiro's fins are completely white. Rarely does a koi fully conform to one of these three sets of criteria nor, provided the effect is pleasing, does it really matter.

The most important koi in this group is the Kumonryu, or 'dragon fish'. It is always Doitsu, always black-and-white, and in the best examples, an interesting wavy white pattern runs symmetrically along either side of the dorsal surface from head to tail. The head may be all-white, all-black or a pleasing combination of the two. Avoid fish with bluish skin, and be aware that young Kumonryu change pattern dramatically as they grow, sometimes for the better, often for the worse. Matsukawabake are also Doitsu, but with a less well-defined pattern that tends to wrap around the body. This is another unstable variety, whose sumi and white are said to reverse according to the seasons – an oversimplification, as the fish is more likely to turn all-white in high temperatures. In transition periods there are really three colours, rather than two, thanks to the blue-black of emerging or receding sumi. The fully scaled version of a Matsukawabake is the Sumi Nagashi, with black scales picked out in white. This pattern may cover the whole body, or contrast against areas of pure white skin. Sometimes the

Left: An example of an accomplished Hageshiro bred in Israel – proof that good koi are not exclusive to Japan. However, in common with many fish from this part of the world, its body shape lets it down.

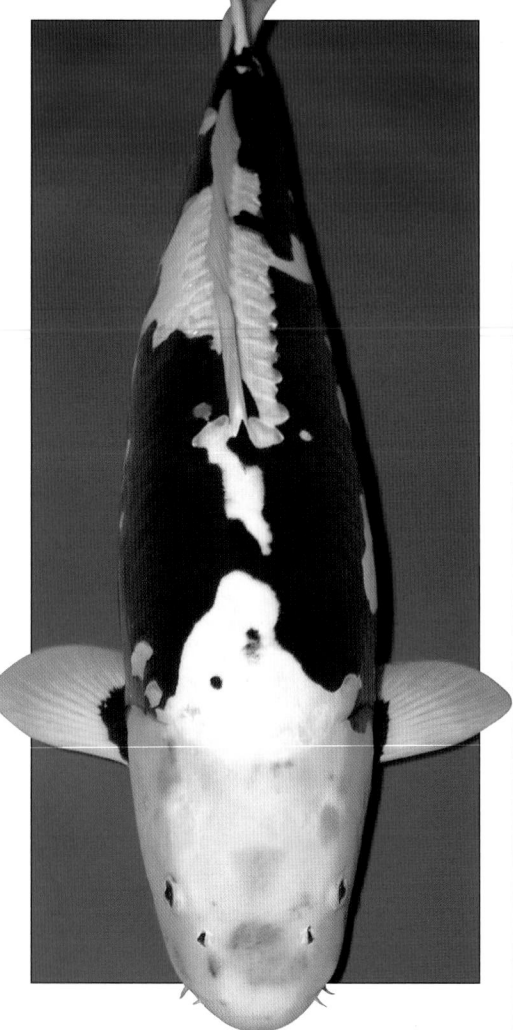

Left: This is a mature Kumonryu. The patterning on this variety can deteriorate with age, but this example shows the classic 'dragon' sumi running lengthways along the dorsal surface.

The velvety black skin is much darker than that of a Magoi.

Sumi is configured in typical Kumonryu fashion.

Balanced pectoral fin sumi is a plus point on this fish.

Above: The distinctive white-tipped tail, dorsal and pectoral fins mark this fish out as a Hajiro – one of the group known as Karasugoi, or 'crow koi'.

tail end of the koi is pure white, and only towards the head is there any black-and-white reticulation.

Kawarimono anomalies

In Japan some koi varieties are placed in Kawarimono, while under non-Japanese show rules, they are benched elsewhere. Prime examples are Goshiki, Koromo Sanke and Koromo Showa (benched Koromo in the West), and Kage Showa/ Kage Utsuri (benched Showa/Utsurimono respectively). The logic is: kage (shadow) sumi may easily be mistaken for emerging sumi, and making a clear distinction is all but impossible, while a Goshiki is only a Koromo in which the robed effect on the pattern extends on to the ground colour. This may occur as the koi ages, so that what is bought as an Ai Goromo later becomes a Goshiki. To save disputes, it is better to bring the two varieties under the same classification.

Above: Where a third colour, hi, is present, a Kumonryu becomes a Beni Kumonryu – still Doitsu and still non-metallic. The metallic version would be a Kikokuryu, and benched Hikarimoyo.

49

HIKARIMUJI

Hikarimuji – single-coloured metallic koi – include the familiar Ogon (formerly spelt 'Ohgon') and the metallic Matsubagoi, whose black scale reticulation is not counted as a secondary colour.

Ogon ancestry can be traced back to 1921, when a Magoi with a gold-striped back was caught from a river in Takezawa, Yamakoshi prefecture, by a gentleman called Aoki. Intrigued by this unusual mutation, he set about fixing it, and after four or five generations of breeding and back-crossing to the original fish he succeeded in producing Ginbo and Kinbo. These dark koi with an overall silver or golden sheen are still thrown in modern Ogon spawnings, but are culled as valueless. So, too, are Kin Kabuto and Gin Kabuto. These have gold or silver-edged scales and a distinctive helmet-shaped head marking. Aoki spawned the first true Ogon in 1946 by running

Swim gym

Ogon may grow fat. To prevent this, install sub-surface filter return pipework, entering the pond at a 45° angle, flush with the walls and pointing slightly downwards. This sets up a circulating current for the koi to swim against, and 'sweeps' solids towards the bottom drains.

Right: *These Purachina (white) and Yamabuki (yellow-gold) Ogon both show the desired clear, broad heads, well-proportioned pectoral fins and overall metallic lustre. Note the almost three-dimensional appearance of the scales.*

a female Shiro Muji (all-white koi) with eight males from the lengthy experimental breeding programme.

Early Ogon were golden, but with a tendency to turn brownish in warm water. They were known as Kinporai, and reputed to look better in the rain than in sunlit pools – an early attempt at marketing hype. Purer and more stable coloration was established when one of these Ogon was crossed with a Kigoi, a very old koi variety. Modern yellow Ogon are known as Yamabuki Ogon.

Rivalling them for beauty are silver-white koi with a deep, dull metallic lustre. These Platinum Ogon, or Purachina, arose in the early 1960s from crosses between Kigoi and the silver-grey Nezu ('Mouse') Ogon. Around the same time, the Cream Ogon became popular. This understated metallic koi, midway between a Purachina and a Yamabuki Ogon,

This Ogon has a graceful and symmetrical body shape for a large fish.

Left: *A beautiful Cream Ogon with just the right body shape. Note that the effect of lustrous pectoral fins is to emphasise the fin rays, which should not show any breaks or deformities.*

Right: *One Japanese word borrowed from the European – 'Orenji' – describes this Ogon with Higoi blood. As in all blends of red and yellow, the exact shade varies between individual examples.*

is enjoying a minor revival at the moment, fuelled by enthusiasts who like their koi to be subtle.

Orange ('Orenji') Ogon resulted from crosses between Higoi and the original yellow metallics, and later with Yamabuki Ogon. Hi Ogon are recorded, but rarely seen.

What makes Ogon so popular? They grow large, and are friendly and unmissable in the pond. More refined tastes favour Go Sanke, but any collection of mainly Kohaku, Sanke and Showa will be enhanced by a few metallics.

Because these are unpatterned fish, Ogon must be exceptional specimens to succeed in shows, with fine skin, even, blemish-free scalation and a clear, lustrous head. The metallic sheen should extend into all the finnage. As the koi grows and the skin stretches, the lighter leading edges of the scales ideally lend it an almost three-dimensional quality.

Mass-produced Ogon are prone to head discoloration and pectoral fins that are too small for the body. They can easily cross the line between 'voluminous' (which is desirable) and 'obese' (which is not). Make sure any fish you choose has both its pelvic fins – missing fins, a genetic fault, can easily be overlooked.

Gin-Rin Ogon

The combination of metallic and sparkling scales in a good Gin-Rin Ogon can be startlingly beautiful. The hallmark of a good specimen is a clear head showing 'Fuji' (as though it has been sprayed with metallic paint which has then developed tiny bubbles).

A metallic fish with Gin-Rin scales – an unlikely but effective combination.

Below: A Gin-Rin Orenji Ogon would be an eye-catcher in any pond. When choosing a fish such as this, first decide its merits as an Ogon. The Gin-Rin scalation is an added bonus.

Doitsu Ogon

In Doitsu Ogon, the enlarged scales along either side of the dorsal fin and along each flank should be neat and symmetrical, and the same colour as the body of the koi. 'Leather', or completely scaleless, Ogons are still benched Hikarimuji. The dull metallic lustre of a good leather Purachina resembles brushed steel.

Matsuba Ogon

Metallic Matsubagoi are benched Hikarimuji. Kin and Gin Matsuba are often seen, not so Orenji and Aka Matsuba (red koi with dark scale reticulation). The pinecone scalation in all these must be well defined, although fish straddling the line between ordinary and Matsuba Ogon are very common.

In Doitsu Matsuba Ogon, the black German scales are aligned as usual, either side of the dorsal fin and along each flank, where they contrast sharply with the metallic body. The orange variety, also known as Mizuho ('Rice Ear') Ogon, is particularly striking.

Below: This Kin Hi Matsuba is a good, though not perfect, example of its variety. The dark nostrils and eye patches let it down, although the head is otherwise clear, with a good lustre.

The scale reticulation on this koi runs down over the flanks, as it should.

Are the pectoral fins of this koi too small for its body? This is a common fault in Hikarimuji.

Above: A Doitsu Kin Matsuba looks worlds apart from its fully scaled counterpart. The stray scales running past the operculum are a fault, and perhaps the metallic lustre is not sufficiently uniform throughout the finnage.

53

HIKARIMOYO

Metallic koi of more than one colour are benched Hikarimoyo (abbreviated from Hikarimoyo-Mono), and result from crossing Ogon, Kin and Gin Matsuba with matt-scaled varieties. This very diverse group excludes metallic Utsuri or Showa, which are benched Hikari Utsuri.

The brash appeal of even poor examples of Hikarimoyo can blind purchasers to their defects – they are koi with seemingly limitless colour permutations and a lustre gleaming up enticingly through the water. But there is a price to pay; metallic scales can tone down underlying pattern, with the result that sumi appears as dark grey, and red as brownish orange. Another common failing is head discoloration, particularly dark lines running from the eyes down to the nose – a throwback to Gin and Kin Kabuto ancestry.

Hariwake

To beginners, Hikarimoyo can only mean Hariwake. These koi display two metallic colours: a platinum base overlaid with either yellow-gold (Yamabuki) or orange (Orenji) markings. Where the second colour is red, a fully scaled fish of this type is known, rather confusingly, as a Sakura Ogon – really a metallic Kohaku – while its Doitsu equivalent is a Kikusui ('water chrysanthemum'), again a platinum fish with overlaid hi. It is not always easy to draw the line between red and orange-red, but it makes no difference to the benching of these koi.

Below: A Yamabuki Hariwake Doitsu. This example has even dorsal scalation, a Kohaku-like pattern and a clear head, all of which combine to give the koi a bright, clear-cut look.

Right: This Kikusui shows a pleasing Inazuma orange pattern balanced by a nose spot. However, the fish lacks volume and the Doitsu scales over the shoulder are rather coarse.

On Doitsu fish without flank scales, the path of the lateral line can be clearly traced.

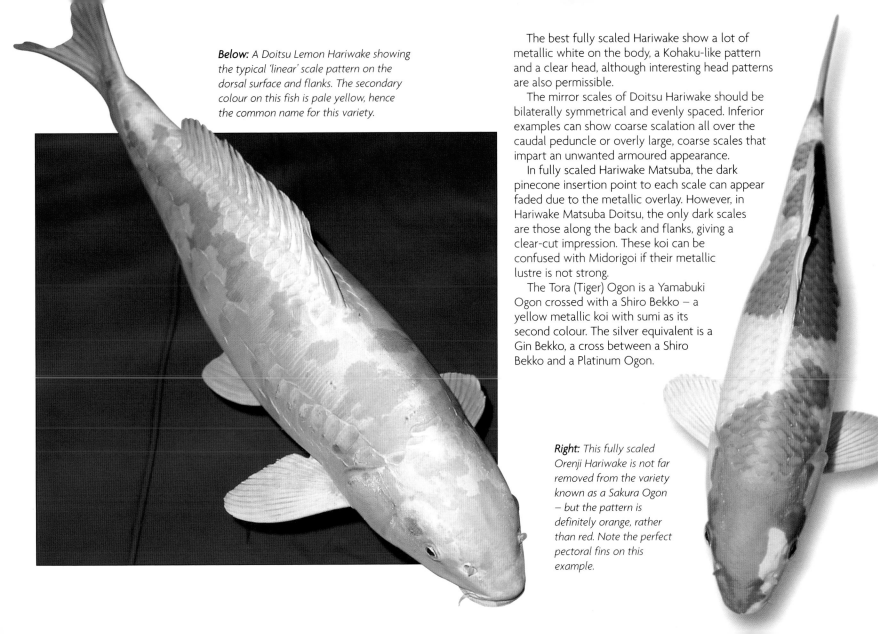

Below: A Doitsu Lemon Hariwake showing the typical 'linear' scale pattern on the dorsal surface and flanks. The secondary colour on this fish is pale yellow, hence the common name for this variety.

The best fully scaled Hariwake show a lot of metallic white on the body, a Kohaku-like pattern and a clear head, although interesting head patterns are also permissible.

The mirror scales of Doitsu Hariwake should be bilaterally symmetrical and evenly spaced. Inferior examples can show coarse scalation all over the caudal peduncle or overly large, coarse scales that impart an unwanted armoured appearance.

In fully scaled Hariwake Matsuba, the dark pinecone insertion point to each scale can appear faded due to the metallic overlay. However, in Hariwake Matsuba Doitsu, the only dark scales are those along the back and flanks, giving a clear-cut impression. These koi can be confused with Midorigoi if their metallic lustre is not strong.

The Tora (Tiger) Ogon is a Yamabuki Ogon crossed with a Shiro Bekko – a yellow metallic koi with sumi as its second colour. The silver equivalent is a Gin Bekko, a cross between a Shiro Bekko and a Platinum Ogon.

Right: This fully scaled Orenji Hariwake is not far removed from the variety known as a Sakura Ogon – but the pattern is definitely orange, rather than red. Note the perfect pectoral fins on this example.

HIKARIMOYO

Metallic Sanke are known as Yamatonishiki. They arose in the 1960s from a complex breeding programme involving a cross between an Asagi and a Kin Kabuto and subsequent introductions of Sakura Ogon blood. The darker the sumi and the more scarlet the hi, the better. Lustrous finnage may or may not show sumi stripes, and in all other respects these koi should resemble true Sanke. A similar-looking fish, the Koshi-nishiki, arose from a cross between a Yamabuki Doitsu and a Gin Showa. The sumi turned out to owe more to Sanke than to Showa lineage, so Koshi-nishiki are now grouped with Yamatonishiki.

Kujaku (or Kujaku Ogon) were first bred in 1960 from Shusui, Kin Matsuba and Hariwake parentage. The result was a metallic platinum fish with black Matsuba scalation overlaying hi, a clear red head, and some blue derived from the female brood koi. Many of these first Kujaku (meaning 'peacock') were Doitsu, from the Shusui influence. Like Goshiki, Kujaku are said to be five-coloured koi, but not all modern fish display white, black, red, brown and yellow. For example, a subvariety, the Beni Kujaku, is predominantly red.

Judging standards for modern Kujaku have become quite flexible. An interesting head pattern is just as acceptable as plain red, yellow or platinum. Still important is a good, even Matsuba pattern from

Right: *A pair of Yamatonishiki, which give a 'feel' for this variety, even though the patterning is very different. See how the sumi is toned down in these metallic koi, suggesting that more can actually be less.*

Above: *The clear metallic saddle, enhanced by broad, lustrous pectoral fins, lends a certain presence to this Doitsu Yamatonishiki. Body volume is not an issue at this early age – the koi should fill out as it matures.*

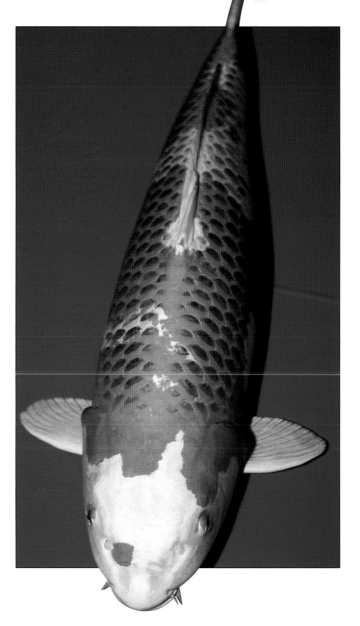

head to tail, and a deep lustre extending into all the finnage. Of all the Hikarimoyo, the Japanese value Kujaku the most highly, because it is so difficult to breed fish that display all the required attributes.

Doitsu Kujaku are sometimes mistaken for the metallic Shusui x Ogon crosses, Ginsui and Kinsui. The difference is in the positioning of the hi which, in the latter, covers the cheeks and flanks, rather than the dorsal surface.

Metallic Ai Goromo (Shochikubai) are quite rare. The reticulated hi is more brown than red, forming a subtle counterpoint to the silver skin.

Given that breeders are understandably tempted to try all permutations of metallic and non-metallic koi to see what arises, Hikarimoyo attracts more than its fair share of new koi varieties. An example is the Kikokuryu, a Doitsu metallic with a helmet-like head pattern not unlike that of a ghost koi. It is over-simplistic to dismiss it as a metallic Kumonryu, because black and silver are not the only colours – hi may also be present, from the black and red fish known as Beni Kumonryu.

Another new 'variety' that has yet to achieve much popularity, is the Heisei-Nishiki – a Yamatonishiki-like koi whose sumi markings owe more to Showa than Sanke without moving it into Kin Showa territory.

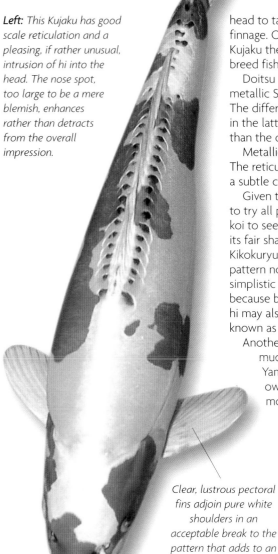

Clear, lustrous pectoral fins adjoin pure white shoulders in an acceptable break to the pattern that adds to an impression of girth where it is most needed.

Left: Were it not for the telltale reticulated mirror scales along the dorsal surface, this Doitsu Kujaku would pass for a Doitsu Hariwake – the pinecone Matsuba scalation is all that sets apart the two varieties.

HIKARI UTSURI

Hikari Utsuri (metallic Showa and Utsurimono x Ogon crosses) proved tremendously popular when they first reached the West. Now their appeal is on the wane, as evidenced by dwindling show entries into this class. It may be that more sophisticated in their appreciation of koi, but more likely, the fall from grace of Hikari Utsuri can be blamed on the toning down of hi and sumi that occurs whenever it is overlain with metallic scales. In all but the very best examples, this results in koi that look washed-out.

Running parallel with this situation is the huge improvement in the quality of matt-scaled Showa and Utsurimono, which need no further gilding to stand out in the pond. Breeders are now back-crossing Hikari Utsuri to the non-metallic side of the partnership in an effort to intensify the hi and sumi while still retaining full lustre.

For some reason, all metallic Showa are known as Kin Showa; there is no such thing as a Gin Showa, even though the koi's prevailing skin colour may be silver. However, Kin and Gin Matsuba are recognised varieties in Hikarimuji.

Left: A Tategoi Kin Showa with marvellous skin and plenty more sumi still to come through. If the black pattern eventually crosses the lustrous face, so much the better. Buying Tategoi is an exciting gamble.

Below: This Kin Showa's hi is toned down by the metallic skin, but the sumi is holding its own. Motoguro fans out into the pectoral fins and balances the head sumi. The koi still has more to do.

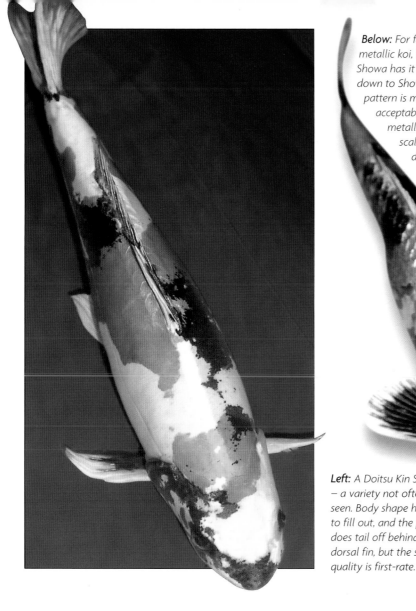

Below: For fans of 'full-on' metallic koi, this Gin-Rin Kin Showa has it all. Taking it down to Showa basics, the pattern is more than acceptable, but do metallic and reflective scales add to or detract from the overall impression?

Left: A Doitsu Kin Showa – a variety not often seen. Body shape has yet to fill out, and the pattern does tail off behind the dorsal fin, but the skin quality is first-rate.

Kin Showa

First and foremost, Kin Showa should measure up to all the usual Showa attributes. Key elements include wraparound sumi, motoguro in the pectoral fins, and an interesting black pattern travelling through the head. Hi and sumi should not tail away, and there must be no congenital mouth or spine deformities. The hi should be dark crimson, rather than the brown it often is, and the sumi as near black as possible. Showa sumi is stronger than that of Sanke, and holds its own better in metallic fish.

All modern Showa pattern variations are permitted in Hikari Utsuri. Metallic Kindai Showa, where white (now silver) predominates, make especially bright koi.

HIKARI UTSURI

Gin Shiro

A metallic Shiro Utsuri is called a Gin Shiro (Gin Bekko are benched Hikarimoyo). The contrast between the black and white areas is toned down, but more apparent in the Doitsu version. The modern taste for smaller areas of sumi suits these koi best, and all-white pectorals, or those with neat motoguro, show off lustre to better advantage than dark finnage.

Kin Hi Utsuri

Kin Hi Utsuri are arguably the most successful Hikari Utsuri. In these metallic Showa, which lack any white, the hi in good specimens remains bright crimson, while the pectoral fins — candy-striped black and silver with a golden overlay — can practically glow. Head sumi is not generally as well-defined as in Shiro Utsuri, and dark nostrils on an otherwise all-red head are a common fault.

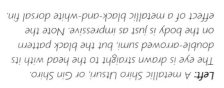

Left: A metallic Shiro Utsuri, or Gin Shiro. The eye is drawn straight to the head with its double-arrowed sumi, but the black pattern on the body is just as impressive. Note the effect of a metallic black-and-white dorsal fin.

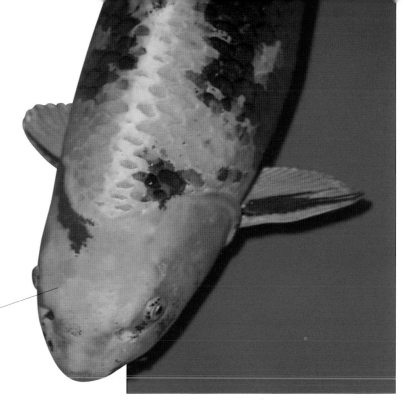

Metallic mongrels

Crosses between normally and metallic-scaled koi can result in attractively patterned pondfish of uncertain lineage. However, all such 'mongrels' (usually home-bred) are still placed in Hikari Utsuri or Hikarimoyo, rather than in Kawarimono, because the latter classification does not include metallics.

Kin Ki Utsuri

The final fish in this classification is the Kin Ki Utsuri – a metallic yellow koi with wraparound sumi. It is usually described as a cross between Ki Utsuri and Ogon, but a more credible parentage would be Yamabuki Ogon/Shiro Utsuri. Matt-scaled Ki Utsuri, although a very old variety, are now hardly ever seen in the hobby.

The bright golden ground colour on good specimens is overlain with Showa-type sumi. The scales appear dark where they enter the skin, blackish gold in the centre, and dark again at the rim – a very subtle and pleasing effect. Any kage (shadowy) patterning that remains into adulthood will not affect the benching of these koi, although it may work against them when they are judged.

Gin-Rin Kin Ki Utsuri offer the added sparkle of reflective scales over a metallic base, but the sumi needs to be very strong to work through this combination. When it does – and as long as the pattern holds up in all other respects – a stunning koi is the result.

Gin-Rin scales are quite distinct from those of metallic koi, although koi such as Gin-Rin Ogon exhibit both types. The flat gleam of metallic scales is caused by the reflective pigment guanine. Kin-Gin-Rin (usually abbreviated to Gin-Rin) scales, on the other hand, have a sparkling deposit over all or part of their surface and, depending on type, may be flat or convex. When they overlay sumi or white they appear silver (Gin), while over hi the effect is golden (Kin). 'Gin-Rin' is frequently mispronounced. The 'G' should be hard, as in 'gate', not soft, as in the spirit mixed with tonic.

Individual sparkling scales first appeared in 1929, on fish owned by breeder Eizaburo Hoshino. He named them 'Gingoke' — another term is 'Dia'. To qualify as Gin-Rin today, a koi should have too many of these scales to be counted accurately as it swims past the observer. The cut-off point is approximately 20. Fewer than that on an otherwise matt-scaled koi can still look very attractive and do not detract from its value. In any case, in the West only Gin-Rin Go Sanke are benched Kin-Gin-Rin. In Japan, Kin-Gin-Rin 'A' covers Go Sanke, and Kin-Gin-Rin 'B' covers all other koi with scales of this type.

If the sparkling deposit is heavy enough, the central area of the scales will feel slightly raised, like the dimples on a golf ball. This is Pearl, or Tsubo, Gin-Rin, also known as Tama-Gin.

The three forms of flat Gin-Rin

Flat Gin-Rin occurs in three forms. In Beta-Gin, the whole surface of the scale sparkles. Beta-Gin is usually found on the abdomen, along the lateral line

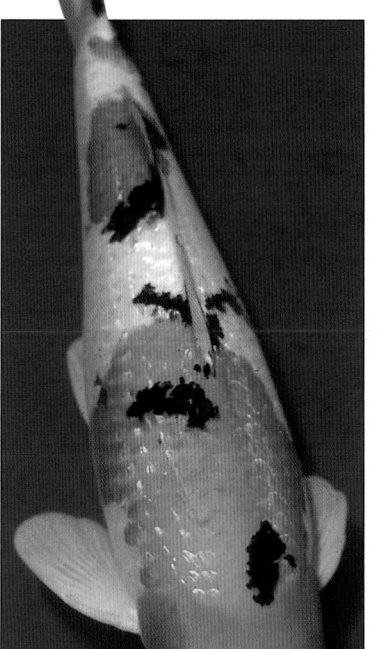

Above: *Anyone would be proud to own this impressive Gin-Rin Sanke. The white saddle with tsubo sumi, the well-placed shoulder marking and neatly aligned sparkling scales all add up to a really class act in koi terms.*

Different scales

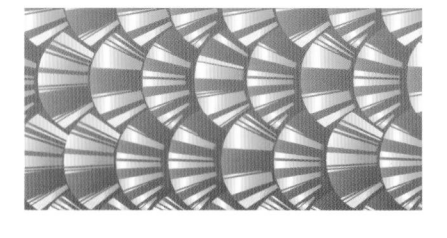

Diamond Gin-Rin *The most striking, yet the least esteemed, form of Gin-Rin is also known as 'Hiroshima Gin-Rin' from its place of origin in southern Japan. It can hide a multitude of sins.*

Kado-Gin *Only the scales' leading edges are iridescent. The amount of shiny pigment must be uniform across all scales. Gin-Rin should extend over the dorsal surface, although often it does not.*

Beta-Gin *Iridescent pigment covers the entire scale surface, not just the leading edges. This type of Gin-Rin is often found in 'borderline' fish; ideally it should cover much of the body.*

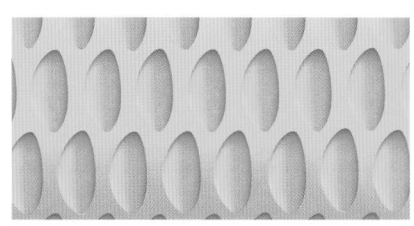

Pearl Gin-Rin *Also known as 'Tama-Gin' or 'Tsubo-Gin'. This type of scale looks best on younger koi. The centre of each carries a raised deposit of iridescence and gives the skin a 3-D appearance.*

Below: There is no doubt that this is a fine Gin-Rin Kohaku, but fish with fewer iridescent scales than this can either be benched in their own variety or add fuel to the ongoing Gin-Rin versus 'Fukurin' debate.

Beneath the glitter, all the Kohaku attributes of this voluminous koi stand up to close scrutiny.

or in individual rows towards the dorsal surface. In Kado-Gin, only the leading edge carries the glistening pigment. The third type, Diamond or Hiroshima Gin-Rin, appeared in 1969 on the Konishi koi farm in southern Japan. In this form, the reflective element radiates out from the root of the scale like the blades of a fan. While such koi have instant appeal to beginners, the Japanese like this type of Gin-Rin least of all. They claim it makes the koi appear flashy and unrefined. Because the leading edge of these scales is often ragged, they can blur hi and sumi patterns, however sharp kiwa and sashi may be. Diamond and Kado-Gin tend to cover the back of the koi, but it is quite possible for a koi to show more than one type on different parts of its body.

Good Gin-Rin should be viewed as a feature that enhances an already beautiful koi, not as something that covers its defects. The fact that Gin-Rin Go Sanke have their own showing class suggests that they would not be able to hold their own against normally scaled fish of the 'Big Three' varieties.

Fukurin scalation

In the past decade, leading breeder Matsunosuke has been deliberately producing Go Sanke said to possess 'Fukurin' scalation. Sceptics write this off as poor quality Kado-Gin, while other hobbyists are equally emphatic that it is not Gin-Rin at all, but a subtle, silky 'shine' that owes nothing to Dia bloodlines. The distinction has to be drawn

somewhere, since Grand Champions at shows are seldom drawn from Kin-Gin-Rin, and 'wrongly' benched koi can thus upset exhibitors in two classes.

Gin-Rin is increasingly found on single-coloured koi, such as Chagoi and Soragoi, 'lifting' them into another dimension. It is a worthwhile attribute, too, on Asagi. Hobbyists who consider the matt version to be somewhat uninspiring may still be drawn to the same koi with an overcoat of sparkling scales.

Right: The increasing popularity of Soragoi (grey koi) is down to breeders producing more of these very understated fish with the added allure of Gin-Rin scales.

TANCHO

Tancho are very much koi for the purist – the Tancho Kohaku, especially, epitomising the Japanese love of perfection in simplicity. This attribute is apparent in several of their traditional art forms, including Bonsai and Zen gardens, with their stark and symbolic arrangements of rocks and raked gravel. What makes an otherwise pure white koi with perfectly circular head hi even more desirable is that good examples are extremely rare. Usually, either the hi lets a fish down in terms of its depth, shape or position, or else the koi's body is somehow at fault – too fat, too thin, or with disfiguring shimis.

The national bird of Japan is the Tancho crane which, like its namesake koi, sports a round, red head marking. There is an obvious tie-in, too, with the Japanese flag, so Tancho koi strike several

Oval Tancho markings are quite acceptable, as long as they balance out the white head and do not stray to one side. Nothing smaller than this would look right.

As perfect as they come, this Tancho marking is the right size and shape, and positioned centrally between the eyes of the koi.

Occasionally, a 'unique' Tancho marking is found. If all other qualities in the koi are good, such a head would draw acclaim and make the fish a winner.

Under enlightened judging standards, this unusual heart-shaped Tancho marking could possibly beat the traditional circular configuration.

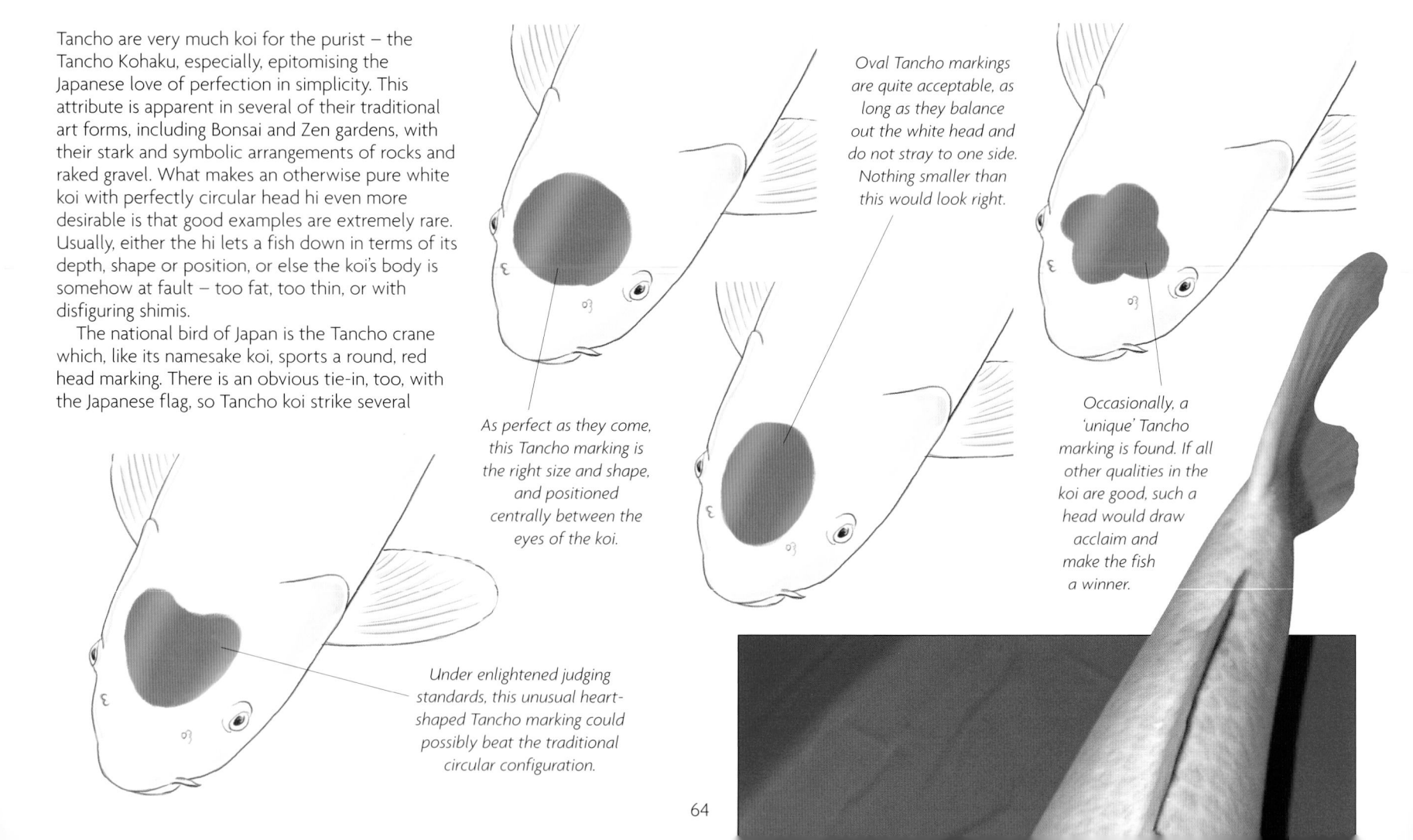

emotional chords simultaneously.

Virtually any koi variety can display a symmetrical head marking loosely described as 'Tancho', and this would not even have to be a red patch; for example, it could just as easily be sumi on a Yamabuki Ogon as hi on a Karasugoi. But the only true Tancho are Kohaku, Sanke and Showa. To qualify for Tancho status, the head hi has to be the only patch of that colour on the fish. The term for a koi with stand-alone head hi and red patterning elsewhere on the body is 'Maruten'. Even red lips (Kuchibeni) would make an otherwise perfect Tancho Go Sanke valueless for showing.

Tancho koi can occur in normal, Doitsu or Gin-Rin form. For benching purposes (in Go Sanke only), Tancho overrides Gin-Rin.

Tancho Kohaku

The classic Tancho Kohaku has a circle of crimson hi sited centrally between the eyes. The more perfect that circle, the more valuable the koi. But standards have been relaxed to a point where Tancho Kohaku with oval, crown-shaped, heart-shaped or other interestingly configured hi are also judged favourably. Whatever form the hi takes, an imaginary line drawn down the centre of the head should perfectly bisect it. Hi slipping down over one eye, like a jauntily worn beret, is fine in Maruten, but not Tancho Kohaku. For every Tancho Kohaku worth the name, many Shiro Muji, and fish with inferior head hi, will result. Other koi, with small additional patches of body hi, are neither good Tancho nor good conventional Kohaku.

Tancho Sanke

Tancho Sanke have head hi complemented by Bekko-type sumi markings on the body and in some or all of the fins. Although small patches of sumi are

Right: *The eye is naturally drawn to the near-perfect hi on this classic Tancho Kohaku, but the fish has other fine attributes – wonderful pectoral fins, good volume and gleaming white skin.*

Tancho tampering

It is not unknown for Tancho koi to be 'doctored' to improve the uniformity of the head marking. This is done by cryo-surgery, and careful inspection will usually reveal the site of the tampering. Rogue individual red scales on the body of Tancho Kohaku can likewise be bleached or scratched off, so let the buyer beware!

permissible on the head of a normal Sanke, a Tancho Sanke's hi should sit on a clear white ground. Many Bekko are thrown from spawnings of this tricky variety.

Tancho Showa

The third type of Tancho koi is really a Shiro Utsuri with additional head hi, but is known as a 'Tancho Showa'. In these fish, the hi is usually cut through by sumi in a classic menware or V-shaped pattern. More wraparound sumi is present on the body. Such koi are less subtle than Tancho Kohaku because their Shiro Utsuri patterning alone is sufficient to delight the eye. The hi is a bonus – a setting sun crossed by the first clouds of night.

The effects of stress

Koi vary greatly in their reaction to being shown. Some take it in their stride, while others are badly stressed by the experience. When this happens, tiny capillary blood vessels under the skin rupture, turning white areas pink. This is especially noticeable on koi in the Tancho classification, and can wreck their chances. Equally frustrating are koi that lose their head hi soon after purchase. The owner of many a Shiro Muji is waiting – usually in vain – for it to return to Tancho Kohaku status.

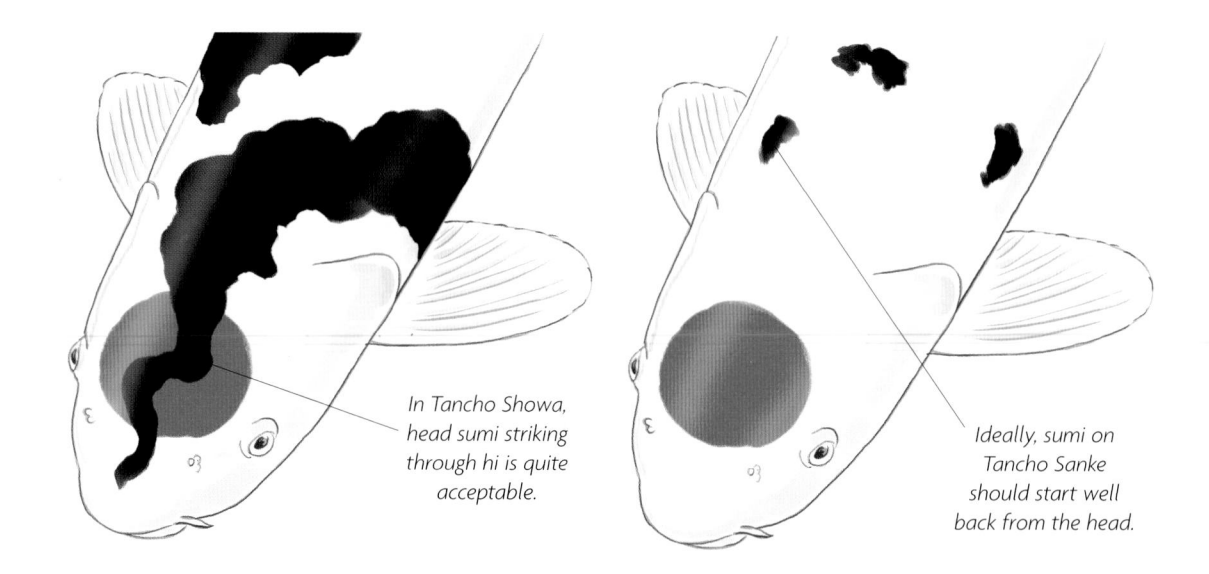

In Tancho Showa, head sumi striking through hi is quite acceptable.

Ideally, sumi on Tancho Sanke should start well back from the head.

Right: The pattern on this Tancho Showa tails off a little, and the head hi wanders over to one eye. Nonetheless, this voluminous koi shows classic head sumi and pectoral fins, and the hi is not overwhelmed but complemented by the intrusion of black.

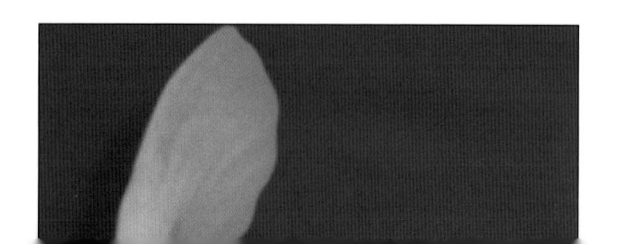

Left: *In Tancho Sanke, the sumi as well as the head hi must be well-placed. This is certainly the case here, and although the Tancho marking flattens towards the nose, it is still nicely symmetrical. If there were any hi on the body of either of these fish, they would cease to be true Tancho.*

67

DOITSU

Today, the word 'mutant' is so much tied in with science-fiction writing that it carries monstrous associations – yet all koi owe their existence to spontaneous genetic changes. Mutations were responsible for the first red or white scales on ancestral black carp bred for food by the Japanese, and later, in Europe, for aberrant scale patterns.

In the wild, mutations are rarely successful because they tend to work against the survival of the animal or, at best, do nothing to enhance its chances of reaching sexual maturity. For example, albinism (where the black pigment melanin is absent) makes fish especially vulnerable to predators. Even if a mutant wild fish does manage to spawn, there is a bottomless gene pool out there to 'dilute' any new physical or behavioural traits and prevent them becoming mainstream. Evolution is a scientific fact, but other than in isolated populations it tends to be a slow process.

Scale mutations

In Europe, producers of carp for human consumption noticed that in any given spawning, some fish would grow much faster than others. These were retained as broodstock in the hope that their offspring would inherit the trait and, indeed, some did. However, this selective breeding programme also resulted in carp whose scales were very different to the norm. So-called 'mirror' carp have a

variable number of enlarged and often reflective scales. 'Leather' carp are practically naked, while linear carp have a double row of scales on the dorsal surface and a single row following the path of the lateral lines.

As well as being easy to prepare for the table, the fast-growing linear carp have played a part in the development of koi. 'Doitsu' (German-scaled) fish came to Japan in about 1907 and were spawned with normally scaled koi. The earliest crossings resulted in Shusui, which are simply Doitsu Asagi.

The Doitsu genetic input is a mixed blessing in koi bred primarily for colour and/or pattern, for while a pure-scaled x linear-scaled cross theoretically produces a 50:50 split, parent koi are likely to be of mixed heritage and an indeterminate number of Doitsu fish will be thrown in any spawning. It is even possible for fully scaled parent koi

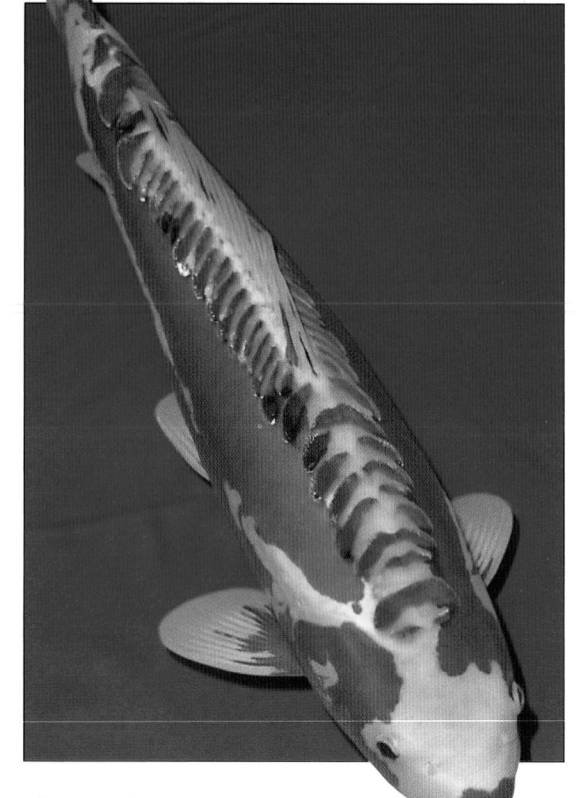

Above: *In the West, Shusui are the only named Doitsu fish to have their own show classification, which they share with fully scaled Asagi. With this amount of red, the fish pictured would be known as a Hi Shusui.*

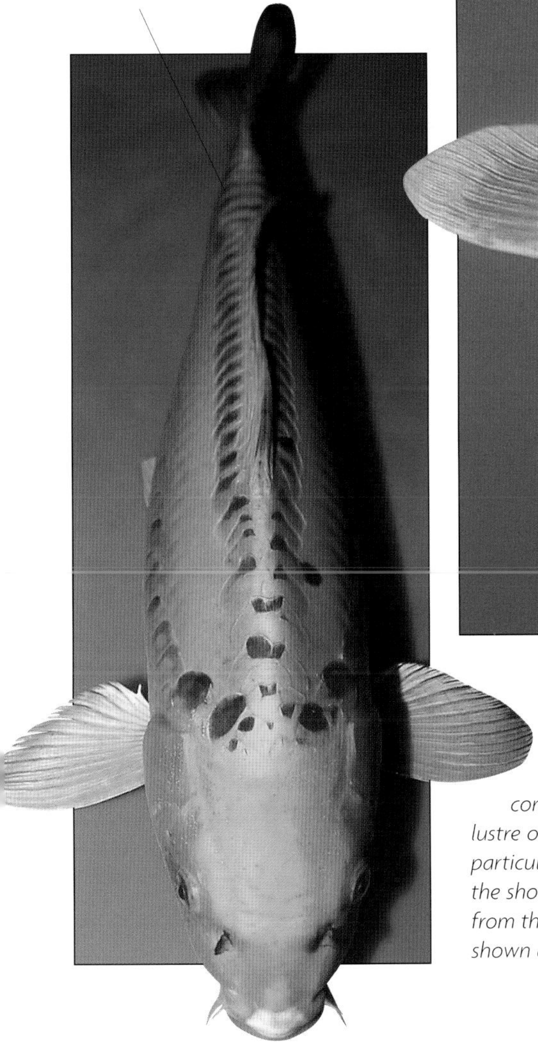

Doitsu scalation must be neat
and even, right along
the dorsal surface
to the tail.

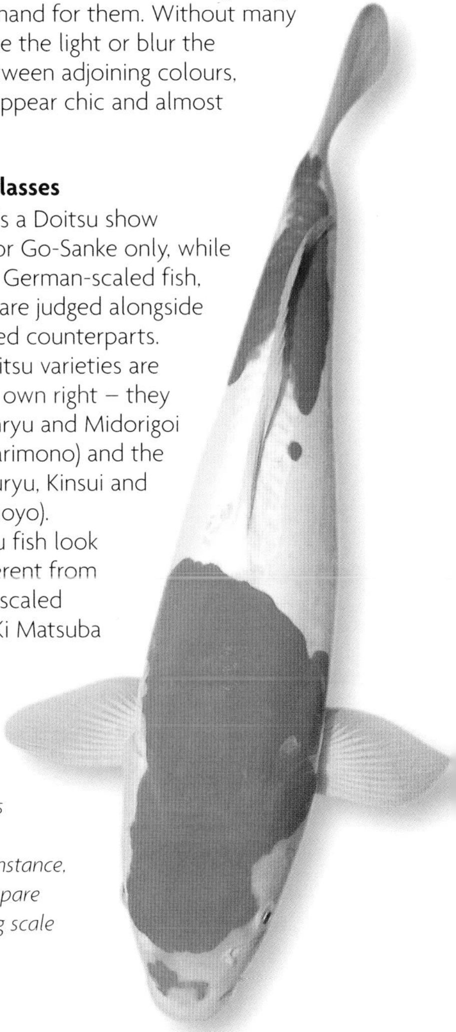

carrying a recessive gene to produce linear-scaled koi, and this is not always what the breeder wants.

The Japanese regard Doitsugoi as rather vulgar and two-dimensional, while still recognising the worldwide demand for them. Without many scales to diffuse the light or blur the boundaries between adjoining colours, these koi can appear chic and almost hand-painted.

Doitsu show classes

In Japan there is a Doitsu show classification for Go-Sanke only, while in the West all German-scaled fish, except Shusui, are judged alongside their fully-scaled counterparts. Only a few Doitsu varieties are named in their own right – they include Kumonryu and Midorigoi (benched Kawarimono) and the metallic Kikokuryu, Kinsui and Ginsui (Hikarimoyo).

Some Doitsu fish look startlingly different from their normally scaled counterparts. Ki Matsuba

Left: *Doitsu Kin Matsuba, a variety that can cause considerable identity confusion. The metallic lustre on this example is particularly good. Note how the shoulder scalation differs from that of the Midorigoi shown above.*

Above: *The translucent quality of the greenish yellow skin of this Midorigoi is typical of this rather rare variety. In response to demand, more of these koi are now being bred, but bear in mind that they tend to turn a muddy greenish brown as they mature.*

Right: *The 'beauty spot' on the body of this Doitsu Kohaku is a nice touch. Note how the enlarged dorsal scales take on the colour of the underlying skin – in this instance, red and white – and compare them with the contrasting scale pattern of a Shusui.*

Doitsu clearly lack pinecone scalation and are much more like matt Kinsui, while Ai Goromo Doitsu have clear hi with only blue-black dorsal scales overlaying the red pattern. The traditional 'robing' effect is absent.

It is debatable whether any Doitsu koi can be fairly judged against fully scaled fish. At top show level, a Doitsu Kohaku would never beat a fully scaled koi of the same quality, but that does not make it a lesser fish. A Doitsu 'A' class for Go Sanke and Doitsu 'B' for the rest would be one solution.

Choosing Doitsu koi

When choosing Doitsu koi, look for neat and evenly placed scalation. The enlarged scales on either side of the dorsal fin should match up left and right, while those on the shoulder should form a pleasing arrangement without being too coarse and overwhelming. There should be no stray mirror scales on the flanks or belly.

There is a type of Doitsu koi known as a 'fully scaled mirror', where the whole body is covered by enlarged scales. These can make pretty pondfish, but are valueless for showing.

Leather koi (also classed as Doitsu) are almost completely scaleless, and this configuration works especially well on metallics, such as Doitsu Purachina. Having a naked or near-naked skin is no handicap to a koi, except that any enlarged scales are prone to catching on obstructions in the pond. Infection can then set in within the scale pocket, and if this results in the scale being lost or removed, the essential symmetry will be lost.

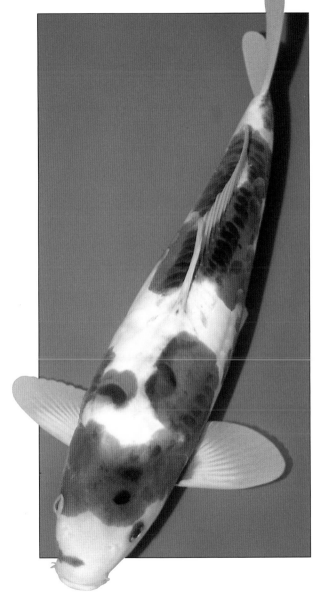

Left: *A young and accomplished Doitsu Goshiki of the modern type, with large areas of white skin. The clear pectoral fins are a major plus point. It will be interesting to see how this fish looks when it is bigger – will more dark pigment appear? The potential for change is one of the fascinations of koi-keeping.*

Above: *If Picasso had been asked to paint a koi, he might well have come up with something like this stunning Doitsu Showa. The fish has perfect white skin on which hi and sumi are equal players, while the body shape is particularly good. This is the kind of perfection breeders strive for.*

Ai Goromo White koi with red Kohaku pattern. Each red scale is reticulated in black or dark blue

Aka Bekko Red koi with black Sanke-type markings

Aka Hajiro Red koi with white-tipped fins

Aka Matsuba Red koi with dark scale reticulation

Aka Muji Non-metallic all-red koi

Aka Sanke Koi with large areas of red unrelieved by cuts in the pattern

Akame Kigoi Red-eyed albino koi

Asagi Koi with a bluish back with reticulated scale pattern. Some red on cheeks, flanks and pectoral fins

Asagi Magoi Forerunner of all modern koi

Right: Classic Asagi, an early, understated koi variety, recognisably close to the ancestral Magoi. Dorsal scale reticulation is particularly good in this example.

Ato sumi Black markings that appear later in a koi's life

Bekko Black Sanke-type markings on a white, red or yellow base

Benigoi Non-metallic, deep crimson koi

Beni Kujaku Predominantly red sub-variety of Kujaku

Beni Kumonryu Kumonryu in which the normally white areas are replaced by hi – a black and red koi of Karasu lineage

Beta-Gin The whole surface of the scale is reflective

Boke Showa Showa with indistinct greyish black pattern

Budo Goromo White koi with purplish patches of black overlaying red in a pattern resembling bunches of grapes

Budo Sanke Budo Goromo with additional solid black markings

Chagoi Non-metallic brown koi

Dia Mutant scales that appear gold over red, and silver over white areas of skin. *See* Gin-Rin.

Diamond-Gin-Rin Reflective pigment that radiates out in a fan shape

Doitsu Koi with no scales other than enlarged scales along the lateral line and two lines running either side of the dorsal fin

Doitsu Ai Goromo The only blue/black scales are the enlarged ones running along the back

Doitsu Hariwake Platinum koi with metallic yellow (gold) markings

Fuji Metallic lustre with tiny bubbles

Fukurin Net effect of lustrous skin around the scales of (usually) metallic koi

Gin Silver

Gin Bekko Cross between a Shiro Bekko and a Platinum Ogon

Ginbo Dark koi with an overall silver sheen

Gin Kabuto Black helmeted koi with silver edges to scales

Gin Matsuba Metallic silver with pinecone scalation

Gin-Rin Koi with reflective silver scales

Gin Shiro Metallic Shiro Utsuri

Ginsui Metallic Shusui with a silver lustre

Godan Five-step pattern

Go Sanke Koi from the Kohaku, Sanke and Showa classes

Goshiki Koi with five-colour pattern made up from red, white, black, light blue and dark blue

Goshiki Shusui Doitsu, non-metallic blue Goshiki

Hageshiro Black koi with white on the head and white-tipped pectoral fins

Hajiro Black koi with white tail tip and white-tipped pectoral fins

Hana Shusui Red in a wavy pattern to give a flowery effect

Hariwake Two-coloured koi with platinum base overlaid with orange or gold

Heisei-Nishiki Doitsu Yamatonishiki with sumi all over the body

Hi Red

Hi Asagi Asagi in which red patterning extends almost up to the dorsal fin

Higoi Red koi

Hikarimoyo Class for all multicoloured metallic koi except Utsuri and Showa

Hikarimuji Class for single-coloured metallic koi

Hikari Utsuri Class for metallic Utsurimono and Showa

Hiroshima Gin-Rin Reflective pigment that radiates out in a fan shape

Hi Showa More than half the body viewed from above is red

Hi Shusui Red extends up over the back contrasting with the dark blue

Hi Utsuri Black koi with red or orange markings

Hon sumi Solid Sanke-type black markings

Inazuma Lightning bolt pattern

Ippon hi Where solid red runs from nose to tail without a break

Kado-Gin Scales where only the leading edge carries the reflective pigment

Kage Shadowy black reticulated marking over white (or red on Hi Utsuri)

Kanoko Dappled, like a fawn (usually applied to stippled hi markings on a Kohaku)

Kanoko Kohaku Kohaku with dappled red pattern

Karasu Koi with matt black fins and body and a white or orange belly

Kasane sumi Black that overlays red

Kawarimono Class for all non-metallic koi not included in any other group

Ki Yellow

Ki Bekko Lemon-yellow with black Sanke-type markings

Kigoi Non-metallic lemon-yellow koi

Kikokuryu Metallic Kumonryu

Kikusui Doitsu platinum koi with metallic orange markings

Ki Matsuba Non-metallic yellow koi with pinecone scalation

Kin Gold

Kinbo Dark metallic koi with an overall golden sheen

Kindai White skin predominates

Kin-Gin-Rin/Gin-Rin Koi with highly reflective gold and/or silver scales

Kin Hi Matsuba Rare red metallic koi with pinecone scalation, also known as Aka Matsuba Ogon

Kin Hi Utsuri Metallic black koi with red or orange markings

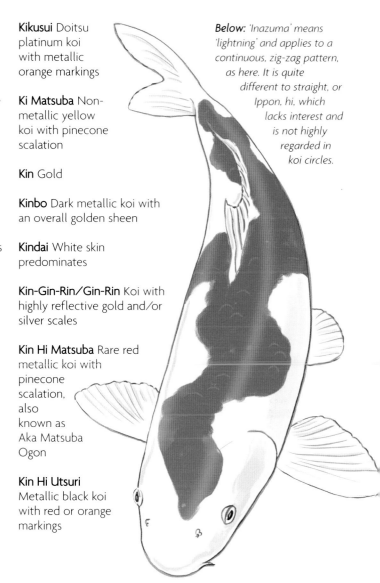

Below: 'Inazuma' means 'lightning' and applies to a continuous, zig-zag pattern, as here. It is quite different to straight, or Ippon, hi, which lacks interest and is not highly regarded in koi circles.

GLOSSARY

Kin Kabuto Black helmeted koi with gold edges to scales

Kin Ki Utsuri Metallic yellow koi with Showa-type sumi

Kin Matsuba Metallic yellow koi with pinecone scalation

Kin Showa Metallic Showa with gold lustre

Kinsui Metallic Shusui with a gold lustre

Ki Shusui Shusui with yellow instead of red coloration

Ki Utsuri Black koi with yellow markings

Kiwa Border of red and white at the rear edge of hi patterns

Kohaku White koi with red markings

Kokesuke Semi-translucent

Komoyo Small flowery hi markings

Koromo Sanke Ai Goromo with Sanke Hon sumi

Konjo Asagi Dark blue fish. Forerunner of modern Asagi

Koromo 'Robed'. Red coloration overlaid with blue or black

Koromo Showa Solid black joins black reticulation over the red

Koshi-nishiki Cross between Yamabuki Doitsu and Gin Showa

Kuchibeni Red lips – literally 'lipstick'

Kujaku (Ogon) Metallic koi with red pattern on a white base and matsuba scalation

Kumonryu Black doitsu koi with some white on head, fins and body

Magoi Ancestral black carp from which all koi were developed

Below: Kujaku are the most variable, and therefore challenging, metallic koi variety. Essential attributes are good scale reticulation, clear head and overall lustre extending into all finnage.

Maruten Kohaku Kohaku with self-contained head marking, plus red elsewhere on body

Maruten Sanke Sanke with self-contained head marking, plus red elsewhere on the body

Matsuba/Matsubagoi Black centre to scale giving a pinecone appearance

Matsukawabake Non-metallic black and white koi, whose pattern changes significantly with season and water temperature

Menkaburi Red extends down to the nose and over the jaws

Menware Strike-through sumi pattern on head of Showa, Utsurimono or Hikari Utsuri

Midorigoi Greenish yellow koi with mirror scales

Mizuho Ogon 'Rice-ear' Ogon. Another name for Orange Doitsu Ogon

Motoguro Solid black coloration in the base of the pectoral fins on Showa and related varieties

Moto sumi Early sumi that remains on the body

Narumi Asagi Asagi with light blue pattern

Nezu Ogon Dull metallic, greyish silver koi

Nibani Unstable secondary red

Nidan Two-step pattern

Nishikigoi Brocaded carp

Right: Shiro Utsuri meet all the requirements of those who like chic and minimalist koi. Sumi should contrast with snow-white skin. Good examples can outpoint Go Sanke for major awards at shows.

Ochiba/Ochibashigure Blue-grey koi with a brown pattern

Ogon Single-coloured metallic koi

Ojime A white caudal peduncle

Omoyo Large imposing hi markings

Orenji Orange

Pearl Gin-Rin Reflective, slightly convex silver scales

Platinum Ogon Metallic white koi (also known as Purachina)

Purachina Metallic white koi (also known as Platinum Ogon)

Sakura Ogon Metallic Kohaku

Sandan Three-step pattern

Sanke 'Three colour'. White koi with red and black markings

Sanke Shusui Doitsu Sanke whose pattern is underlaid with the blue back of the Shusui

Sashi Overlap of red and white scales at the forward edge of hi patterns

Shimi Undesirable individual dark brown or black scales on areas of ground colour

Shiro Bekko White koi with black Sanke-type markings

Shiro Matsuba White koi with black pinecone reticulation

Shiro Muji All-white, non-metallic koi

Shiro Utsuri Black koi with white markings

Shochikubai Metallic Ai Goromo

Showa Black koi with red and white markings

Showa Shusui Doitsu koi with intermediate markings showing elements of both varieties

Shusui Doitsu Asagi

Soragoi Plain blue-grey koi

Sumi Black

Sumi Goromo White koi with red patterns lightly overlaid with black

Sumi Nagashi Koi with black scales picked out in white

Taisho Sanke/Taisho Sanshoku Full names for Sanke

Taki Sanke Asagi koi with white line dividing areas of red and blue on the flanks

Tama-Gin Another name for Pearl Gin-Rin

Tancho Circular red spot on head. No other red on body

Tancho Sanke Sanke with a patch of red confined to the head

Tancho Showa Showa with a patch of red confined to the head

Tategoi 'Unfinished' koi of any age that should continue to improve

Tora/Tiger Ogon Ogon with black markings; metallic equivalent of Ki Bekko

Tsubo-Gin Another name for Pearl Gin-Rin

Tsubo sumi Black on white skin

Utsurimono Black koi with white, red or yellow markings

Yamabuki Yellow-gold

Yamatonishiki Metallic Sanke

Yondan Four-step pattern

Yotsujiro Black koi with white head, pectoral, dorsal and caudal fins

INDEX

Page numbers in **bold** indicate major entries; *italics* refer to captions and annotations; plain type indicates other text entries.

CREDITS

Practical photographs by Geoffrey Rogers © Interpet Publishing.

The publishers would like to thank the following photographers for providing images, credited here by page number and position: B(Bottom), T(Top), C(Centre), BL(Bottom Left), etc.

Shunzo Baba (Kinsai Publishers Co. Ltd., Tokyo): 16-17(R), 17(BL), 21(C), 37(L), 48(C), 48-9(R)
Nigel Caddock, Nishikigoi International: Title page, 19(R), 20, 21(R), 22-23(R), 24, 25(C,R), 26, 28(R), 29(L,C), 30(C), 30-31(R), 33(R), 35, 38(R), 40(L,R), 41(L), 42-43(R), 44-45(R), 46-47(L), 47(R), 48(L), 50, 51(L), 54(R), 55(R), 56(R), 57(L), 58(C), 59(C), 60-61(L), 60(C), 64-65, 66-67(R), 68-69(C), 69(L,R), 70-71(R), 71(L)
Andrew McGill: Copyright page, 15(BR), 28(L), 33(L), 34, 37(R), 38(C), 41(R), 42(C), 43(L), 45(L), 51(R), 52, 53(C,R), 54(C), 55(L), 56(C), 57(C), 58-59(R), 59(L), 60-61(R), 62, 63(L,R), 66-67(L), 68(R), 72, 74, 75
Tony Pitham (Koi Water Barn): 8(BL,BR), 9, 15(C), 22(C)

Illustrations by Stuart Watkinson © Interpet Publishing.

The publishers would like to thank Koi Water Barn, Chelsfield Village, Kent, for their help.